THERE IS NO MAGIC BUTTON.

Practical tips to stop drinking.

Stephanie Chivers.

Forward

This is an excellent book for anyone who wants to get back in the driving seat in their own lives. As Stephanie says in the introduction:

This book is for you if you want to gain some control of your life. If you are too busy, tired, eating too much rubbish, not doing enough exercise, drinking too much or life has just got difficult for you. Maybe you are even participating in other bad habits: smoking, recreational drugs, gambling, shopping too much and Facebook taking over your life, the list goes on.

Sounds like me and probably you or someone you know, most of us find that at some point in life we get so overwhelmed or stressed, we lose focus and start behaving in a way that we really don't want to.

What I love about Stephanie's approach is that it is entirely positive, for anyone who thought they were an alcoholic, doomed to be forever a gambling loser, or an obese sugar head, she shows that by implementing the tools and techniques in the book you can change and the change can be fast. I was in the music business for many years. In that 'sex and drugs and rock n roll' environment, I've known several people who have been to AA meetings year after year, who have been in and out of rehab and given up drugs many times only to go straight back to them the second the going gets tough. I've known people who didn't make it because they felt they never could get the help they needed to conquer their addictions. What's different about this approach is it offers lasting change because it comes from within you.

The book includes an insight into Stephanie's own story, this isn't just a do-gooding counsellor 'talking at ya' but someone who has experienced the pain and the shame of finding herself arrested, wondering just where it all went wrong. Her recovery though was remarkable and entirely without conventional intervention. The book includes other stories too of people who have been there done it, got the T shirt, and what's clear is that it really doesn't matter what your 'addiction' or 'issue' is, there is light at the end of the tunnel and Stephanie shines the light for you get there fairly effortlessly.   As the title says **There is no magic button**, but 'whatever your bad habit is the **good news is you weren't born doing it, you have learnt it and if you have learnt it you can UN learn it!!'** .

This is an easy-to-read, incredibly helpful and inspirational book which will undoubtedly help people reclaim their lives. Despite there being no 'magic button' Stephanie has created something really quite magical with this book and this programme. It comes highly recommended.

Janey Lee Grace is the author of Look Great Naturally without ditching the lipstick and offers media training.
www.janeyleegrace.com

Introduction

This book is for you if you want to gain some control of your life. If you are too busy, tired, eating too much rubbish, not doing enough exercise, drinking too much or life has just got difficult for you. Essentially we are going to start with alcohol but as you know that's just the beginning.

I get asked so many questions all the time, so I thought I would put some of the answers into a book. I can't fit all of it into 1 book, so maybe there will be another one. For now, this book will:

- Give you practical things you can do to help yourself.
- Increase your understanding of why you are doing what you are doing.
- Motivate you.
- Foster the belief that you can change.

This will allow you to start making small changes in your life today.

It won't take up too much of your time, the things you will learn in it you can apply to your everyday life. And sometimes it's just hearing about other people's stories that can inspire you to make changes.

The changes don't have to be big but if you start doing them every day you will begin to feel better. You will start to:

- Feel more in control.

- Sleep better.
- Feel healthier.
- Create some space to figure out what you want and live your life.

If there is one thing I have learned since I have been paying attention; and I have been paying attention for some time now, watching and listening to people. Is that anything is possible, for anyone. Yes, that means you as well. I have seen it, I promise. People from all walks of life and backgrounds, they have made changes. They've cut out their bad habits and addictions that were taking them away from doing what they really want to do (sometimes you are so far away from what you want to do, you have forgotten). When they did this, it cleared the way for so much more. Just imagine how much time and energy you will have!

Read this book all the way through once, consume it, make a note of the bits that really work for you, interest you. Then once you have read it all, start again and do the work.

This book isn't saying stop (well it may do so at points), or reduce, or moderate. It's your choice. Obviously, I want you to be happy and healthy, I know the more alcohol free days you have the better you will feel. When people drink less, or take a break, they achieve so much more. Essentially this book is about teaching, helping and inspiring you to live your life, in whatever form works for you.

"Change is possible for you".

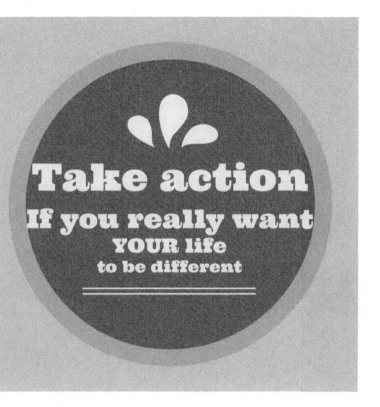

Contents

1.What This Book is About and Why

What Do I know?

Ever since I have been a child I have listened to people talk about their lives. As a little girl, I would sit playing my imaginary games, all the time listening to women talk. Talk about their relationships, their children, love, families, it's just something I have always done. An old friend of mine calls me a listener because people just come to me and start telling me their story.

I love it, life and the stories that surround us. The stories have patterns, repeating patterns that talk to us (if we listen) and there are life lessons in the stories that we can use in our own lives to help us and to give us strength.

There have been times in my life where I have really struggled and I have found solace, strength and guidance in the books of other people lives. It's just life after all, doing its thing, it's twists and turns. Like a good plot in a movie, sometimes you just have to sit tight and trust that something good will come out of it and there will be good moments along the way.

This quote sums it up really well:

Life is amazing and then it's awful,
then it's amazing again,
and in between the amazing
and the awful,
its ordinary mundane and routine.
Breathe in the amazing,
Hold on through the awful,
and relax and exhale during the
ordinary. That's just living,
heart-breaking, soul healing,
amazing, ordinary life.
And it's breathtakingly beautiful.
L R Knost

This book is about habit, essentially you weren't born doing it, so if you have learnt it, you can UN learn it. It really is that simple. It's about how you can start making small changes now, right this minute and then keep doing them until they become a habit.

If you drive think about when you first learnt how to drive. It was probably awkward, you didn't know what you were doing, which pedal was which, so much to think about in one go. But you persevered, you kept going, because you wanted to learn to drive. Because it gave you something: freedom, more job choices, easier time with the kids or maybe you just wanted to get out and about, so many reasons why. You kept learning because you wanted something from it, you had something to aim for. Freedom maybe.

Also, when you start a new job with a new routine, you have to get up early. Initially, it's hard then after a while you just wake up anyway, it started off being difficult, you kept doing it, then it just happened.

Habit is also about you, what YOU can change, what you can control. It puts you at cause, not effect. Now this is important. Are you living your life like a ping pong? I know I did for quite sometime. Bouncing from one thing to the next, not really paying attention.

I am passionate about making sure you have access to good information that gives you everything you need to live the life you want. Change is possible, for anyone. Yes you! I will keep saying it. I can't give you everything in one book, but I am going to give you enough to get started and for most of you that will be enough.

One of the many other things I have learnt from myself and working with others is what you are capable of when you stop spending time on your bad habits. Maybe you spend your time drinking regularly, or just too much at the weekends. When you drink that's what you are doing: drinking, not very much else, but also it is effecting your health, weight, sleep, mood, finances and many other things. Maybe you just feel sluggish and not very good about yourself. I guarantee if you stop drinking for a little while or significantly reduce you will feel so much better: sleep better, lose weight, feel healthier, get a spring in your step, improve your mood and think of the money you will save.

With the thousands of people I have worked with, across the board, it's a no brainer: people stop drinking for a while and they feel so much better. There are so many benefits! 9 out of 10 people feel better. Those that don't are sometimes people who have an underlying mental health problem, or childhood trauma and life was difficult before they started drinking and they drink to manage those problems. If this is you, if you stop drinking and you get all the basics in place, you know make the changes, but even after 3 months you are still struggling, please get help, professional help. There are some great therapists out there, there is no need to suffer. Drinking will only make your problems worse.

Imagine what you can do if you feel better emotionally, physically and you have more time available in your life. It clears space for you to fill it with something you want to do.

I practice what I preach, I use the techniques I have learnt to help me live my life the way I want to. But I am definitely not perfect.

If you have learnt it,
You can unlearn it.

My story

There are several things that have made a difference to my life. But coaching and NLP (Neuro linguistic programming) are the techniques that have really made a difference and continue to do so for me. There has also been some education and information along the way that has helped. Learning about the facts (that bits really important) about alcohol, units, health risks and its impact on behaviour. This has been a big motivator for me, remembering this. In my day to day work and life I repeat a lot of this information daily so it acts as a reinforcement for me. Repetition is the mother of success, as long as the information is good. Although I know a lot about the 12-step approach and have a lot of respect for it, it didn't sit well with me personally. I don't want to have a disease, I don't want to label myself as an addict, and I don't want to say that I am in recovery. **I am a person that has learnt skills that enable me to have choice and live the life I want.** I know what I have done wrong, I can't change the past, it doesn't support me to repeat it and feel the guilt and shame. However, I can be better here and now and that feels good. I think coaching and NLP has worked for me because it made sense to me and ultimately that is what any support is about, if it fits for you and makes sense, use it. It makes sense to me because it has taught me to understand who I am but also more importantly it has given me the tools to change the bits of me that aren't working properly.

I have a story of change; some people would call it recovery. I have a big thing about the language we use. For me it's more about how I changed my behaviour and then in turn, my life, for the better.

I don't call myself an addict either, I don't like that word. And I am guessing a lot of other people who are struggling with their drinking don't see themselves as addicts either. I have been around alcohol and drugs since I was a teenager, I suspect most people my age grew up like that. However, for us it continued. I used drugs and alcohol and behaved badly at times throughout different periods in my life. Sometimes I had a lot of fun, but I also made some very bad choices as a result of my emotional state due to my lifestyle; I wasn't paying attention. Now I only have an occasional drink and I've had a long period of complete abstinence, which I strongly believe in to get you started. Very early on after my big change, I noticed the difference in my emotions. How I could see and feel things clearly, and the clarity was and still is amazing. I very rarely get confused or am a slave to my emotions. I get a kick out of being alcohol free 99% of the time.

My story of change started with one of the worst and best days of my life. It started off as the worst obviously and in that clichéd way I hit my bottom, my low point. Everyone has one and it's at different levels for all of us. Mine was a short stay in custody just before Christmas. I had drunk a huge amount (however I had been drinking daily for a while).

I didn't feel drunk as I had a high tolerance due to the regular drinking. I was arrested on a drink drive charge or drunk drive charge depending on where you live. And I am not proud to say it, it wasn't the first time I had driven under the influence of alcohol and other substances over the years.

Initially I was furious, "how dare they arrest me, who did they think they were?" That was the alcohol speaking, then came the realisation they weren't going to let me out. It hit me. What had happened to my life, how had I ended up there, how had I let things get this bad? In that moment, I took full responsibility for my behaviour. It was my fault, all of it. I had got me there, no one else. I was devastated, the guilt kicked in as I have 2 children. I am a mum, with an ex-husband willing to do anything to get back at me and I had just given him everything he needed. I was done for.

The police said that because I was so far over the limit I was looking at a 3 month prison sentence. I was petrified. I hardly survived in a cell, let alone 3 months. I would lose my children, my job, and my house, everything I had worked so hard to keep.

Bizarrely at the time and at many other points in my life I have had many successes as well, I went up and down like a roller coaster. The success at that time was just starting my NLP practitioner course. (I know, try not to laugh too much at the double standards of my life). But it's an important point as so many people live like this, great jobs, great parents, but parts of their life are chaos, or just not working.

I had discovered NLP (neuro linguistic programming) when I was in my early 20's. A friend of mine was dying and was receiving free therapy to help him with the process. The therapy was NLP and he would come home and tell me all about it. I was fascinated and it made perfect sense to me. How the way you think about things affects your life, but you have to, believe it as well. I read books and did some training courses. Doing the courses and learning started to change me. This wasn't my motivation initially; I was just following my heart. I had a strong pull to this method.

At the point where I got arrested I was awarded some funding and just started my NLP practitioner, something I had wanted to do for a long time. I had worked hard to get there.

On the first day of my training the trainer had my number. I nearly didn't start the course, as I had been out the night before and drank too much, I was late and hungover, which is not conducive to learning.

When I got out of custody I called him, it was a very simple quick call.

"Please help me, I can't do this anymore", He asked me what was happening, I told him "I am ruining my life and I want to stop, I don't know what's wrong with me, it's like some sort of self-sabotage mission".

He agreed to come and see me a few days later. He spent 30 minutes with me using NLP techniques. That was it. I had had enough, I wanted to change, but didn't know how.

He gave me a kick start, then I worked at it. I have a good understanding of addiction; I have been around it from the age of 15. I have friends who had stopped. I knew what I needed to do. I restricted myself, I stayed away from the action, kept myself safe, and I did this for quite a long time. I did relapse massively a few days after, then again, a couple of years later. However now it is no longer an issue. I can drink occasionally but I have respect for it, I know if I let myself I could easily drink every day, but I don't let myself, because I don't want to live like that, it's a waste and I choose not to feel like that.

I applied myself to my job and my training and did really well, I became a better mother and focused on my children and they gave me hell for years. I did up my home, paid off my debts, stayed away from the men with lots of free booze and fun for me. I discovered partner dancing and that became my thing. I became a drug and alcohol worker, a bloody good one and really worked at it. I am a master practitioner of NLP and a coach now. I love my work, I love helping people to live happier healthier lives, it's a buzz.   It wasn't all plain sailing though, my ex-husband continued to make me pay and made my life extremely difficult for years. But living without alcohol in my life was incredibly satisfying because I no longer enabled him to get the better of me. Because I was straight, clear, in charge of my emotions and strong in myself.

I know who I am.

I continue to apply the techniques I have learnt in my training and practice and push myself to be the best I can be, but I know that I need to be careful. Always checking my blind spot!!! I love alcohol, I like the taste, I like how it feels, however I like it too much and let's be honest a lot of people do. It's just when I drink I am an idiot and I do stupid things I would never do when I am not drinking. It's also highly physically and psychologically addictive. So, if you like it and get a taste for it, you are just going to want to do it a lot, it's just one of those things. Same with any drug.

The information I have is based on my training, working with amazing people, what I have learnt and applied to my own life. But also from having supported, taught and watched 1000's and 1000's of people make changes and what it took for them to do so. This book contains what I have learnt, well some of it anyway.

Falling down
is part of life.
Getting back
up is living.

2. Life today

There seems to be something happening today, we are all so busy, women especially. We have gone from our mothers being stay at home mums (not all of them I know) and our dads working a lot, to women who can have it all. But guess what? It's very tiring having it all. I am a big fan of living life on your terms and if you really want it all go for it, I am not going to stop you. But for some of us it can be too much trying to deal with everything life throws at us whilst trying to excel at everything: children, work, partners, houses, illness, divorce, death, family, school, friends, the list goes on. When we get busy and tired, whatever the reason, it's all too easy to slip into bad habits, we are not paying attention and our primary focus is to just keep going, move on to the next thing, get it done. The washing, cooking, cleaning and so on and so on. Rinse, repeat. Write more lists.

And in between the things that you can plan for, life just happens as well: death, divorce, difficult relationships, difficult children, ill children, difficult relatives, financial problems and on and on. "Normal" life can be busy but throw a curve ball in there and things can get really challenging.

Maybe you are: trying to have it all, prove something, caught up in putting others first, not prioritising yourself, making bad decisions, or have just got into bad habits.

It doesn't really matter why, the important thing is you can do something to start making changes.

If you are reading this book, it's because you want to start changing your drinking habits, it doesn't matter how you got here. **The important thing is here and now and what you are going to do about it.**

It all begins with small changes: do something for yourself, sleep a bit more, learn how to relax, eat healthier, drink less, give up smoking, exercise. The drinking less will definitely help with all of this, but more of that later.

Start with making time for this, this book, what you are going to learn, you are going to have to let some of the other stuff go.

Make space for you, just a little bit, it will be worth it I promise.

Here is the thing, there are only 24 hours in a day, you have to sleep, trust me you do (I tried this one before, it creeps up on you if you don't.) You can only do so much; you are only human. Sleep is so good for us.

So be prepared to let some of the other things go and make time for you, to make changes. When you get a grip on your bad habits, it will be so worth it. When you do this, you free up so much time and energy, you can then think about what you want to do with your time. Make space, it's amazing what happens when you do.

Also, be aware of the busyness trap, as this is also a bad habit. We are going to talk about drinking, food and other things that stop us from being the best we can be. But if you are too busy that is a bad habit in itself.

Be honest, is this you? If it is, be prepared to let go of some things, so you can do this.

When you are
overwhelmed, tired or
stressed the solution
is almost always...... less.

Get rid of something,
lots of somethings.

bemorewithless.com

Janes story

I first met Jane about 5 years ago. She had been a heavy stimulant user in her 20s so had been used to being very thin. She knew it was an unhealthy thin, but all the same, there is something about what we are used to. How it feels to be empty. I have worked with many drug users and drinkers who have really struggled with this. They want to stop, they can stop, they feel so much better, look better, and everything is good. But the feeling of having food in your stomach is different. I know this sounds ridiculous but it is very real for some people.

She didn't want to use stimulants again, it made her feel crazy and she didn't like herself on it. She was also drinking a lot at that point as well. This is something else that can happen to people who were recreational drug users in their late teens and twenties. They stop and feel better, but then move on to alcohol just for the simple reason its legal. However, as you will learn in this book, or hopefully you know, alcohol is one of our most harmful substances. It is also highly addictive, readily available and socially acceptable. An easy one to move onto, innocently as well.

The reason Jane came to see me initially was because she was feeling horrible because of her weight. However, we uncovered a few other things. For her, it was understanding that the way she used to live wasn't real, she definitely didn't want to live like that again. It was about relearning. How do people eat, sleep and exercise in normal life? Learning about nutrition, what foods were good, when to eat and how often, exercise. Figuring out what worked for her was key.

Jane went on to learn about the effect her drinking was having. Understanding that this was contributing to her weight and emotional issues was really important. Once she understood the pattern, she was able to cut back. She then noticed that when she didn't drink she felt so much better about herself. She had more energy, was more able to exercise and when she exercised she felt better about herself, whether she lost weight or not. What was important to her was how she felt, learning how to make her life work so she felt good, instead of bad.

Once we had worked through the weight concerns, the negative emotions, drinking, getting into a routine, learning about food and exercise. It became apparent that underneath all of this was her being so busy it was completely ridiculous. She was beyond shattered and would use food and coffee to keep her going, rather than listen to her body and slow down, look after herself. She was unable to prioritise herself as she was putting everyone else first.

Jane had a pattern from early childhood (she was the eldest of a large family) of helping, being the one that got things done, working hard. That is how she got her pay offs, this is how she felt love, by doing things for others. She was co-dependent and needed to be needed. This was at her core. She could do all the other things within reason, eat healthily, drink less, exercise, but then her busyness would creep in and she would be prioritising her partner, the children, her family, pretty much anyone before herself.

Busyness is a constant balancing act for Jane, tweaking, adjusting, grabbing bits of routine for herself so she feels ok.

3. What's the Big Deal with Change?

The one thing I can guarantee is that everything will change. Life is changing all the time even right this moment. It's part of life and nature to be constantly growing and learning. However, some people fear change and really struggle with it, finding it hard to let go of the past and embrace the new, whatever it is. A large part of this is about habit, what we get used to and not necessarily the good things either.

Take the mum who has looked after her children for 18 years and what feels like all of a sudden, (it isn't sudden from the moment they are born we are letting go) the children don't need you anymore. You have gone from your whole life revolving around these other humans; your every decision is about them from the moment you wake, until the moment you go to bed. To only having to look after yourself. All of a sudden you have a lot more time. How you live your life significantly changes, if you are not working you no longer have to even get up, if you work you can stay at work longer (not always a good thing), because you don't have to be home at a certain time, to cook a healthy meal every night. There are so many things that become different in your day to day life. It isn't all focussed around other people. Obviously, this is a big change for a lot of people, but it is a big change made up of a lot of little ones. From the outside looking in it can seem simple; the lady just needs to think about what she wants to do with her life and start doing it. But she may have never been able to make those kinds of choices for herself.

Sometimes we know change is coming: a new job, moving, relationships, children leaving home and we don't want it to happen. Maybe it's not your choice. For example, when contracts change or business's get bought out by someone else and your role is changing. You like your current job and you don't want it to change, but it's out of your control. Choice is a big thing for people, so it's finding where you can find the choice within a situation. So, you can: choose to stay and accept the changes, choose to leave and get another job or you can choose to stay and feel upset and angry about the changes if you want. If you choose to accept the changes, it's accepting it for what it is, and finding things in the new situation that work for you. If you choose to stay and yet you are unable for whatever reason to let go of your negative feelings please go and get some help. You suffer more than anyone in this situation. It will also affect your colleagues and your productivity, which will only make you continue to feel worse.

Sometimes people like to feel sorry for themselves. They feel justified in their negativity and wallow in it. If this is you give yourself a time frame. How long are you going to be angry and why? What is the benefit of this? Sometimes it can be because you want to be right. Your partner left you for another women/man, you feel justified in your anger, and they have been seeing each other for a long time. He/she definitely isn't coming back and in reflection it wasn't a great relationship. It's just you didn't have a choice, he/she left, you are hurt and angry. That's normal, but not if you stay there. It doesn't benefit anyone, least of all you.

I am sure you have noticed as well, being right doesn't win you any prizes. No one comes along and gives you an award and says there you go that was a terrible thing that happened to you, they were wrong and you were right, it must be so because all your friends and family agree. So, in some ways it is irrelevant. How you feel and how you live your life is what matters. Remember: no one is coming to save you, even if you are right!!!!

When I was in my early 20's I was in partnership with a friend. We had a good business; we worked well together even if it was a little volatile at times. But it was a good creative working relationship. As things got more volatile it became harder for the people around us. It was easy for me to be pushed out; I made it easy for others. Rather than embrace the natural change I kicked against it, felt angry and hurt, I enrolled people in my plight as I felt justified as I was right and they were wrong!! However, after some time I started another business and made contacts on my own, one of these contacts turned out to be very profitable for myself and the other company. The benefits I received from this collaboration where far greater than anything I would have received in the other partnership. I wasted time on feeling hurt and right, because I chose not to see the benefits in the change. Be really aware of this. I, made it difficult for me, I, made it last longer, I, stayed in the negative horrible angry feelings, by constantly thinking about it and perpetuating it

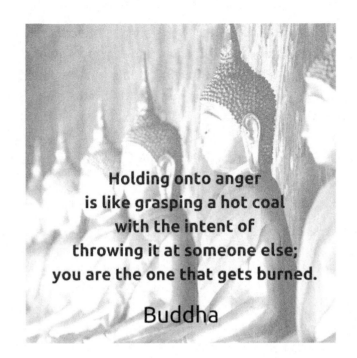

Holding onto anger
is like grasping a hot coal
with the intent of
throwing it at someone else;
you are the one that gets burned.

Buddha

Someone once said to me, the person with the greatest flexibility determines the outcome. It took me a long time to understand this. What it meant and what it means to apply this practically.

4. How Do People Change?

People change in many ways and for many different reasons. Change happens naturally as a part of life. As I have already said change is happening all the time.

The seed is planted, it rains, and the sun shines and it starts to grow. It very rarely just stays a seed in the ground unless there is something fundamentally wrong with it. We change as we grow from babies to children to teenagers and adults, constantly changing our minds, bodies, values, identity. A lot of it is natural, just part of life.

Sometimes people resist this: the teenager who doesn't want to be a grown up, the student who doesn't want to go out to work or the mum who doesn't want to be her own person.

Sometimes other people want us to change, if we are lucky they tell us, but unfortunately sometimes we learn from feedback from the way they interact with us (if we are listening that is). Maybe we are drinking too much and we are difficult to be around, maybe we are insensitive or rude and don't realise the impact of our communication.

As a manager in an alcohol treatment service we would see a lot of men who had been sent by their wives. (I am not being sexist, it's just what happened). Because the wife wants them to stop drinking: for health reasons, for the sake of the relationship, parenting, financial issues there can be many reasons. Quite often the man would be honest and say my wife wants me to stop that's why I am here. Now most people in the profession would say there is no point him being there, the motivation must come from him. But I would argue that, saying that he is there in front of you, he is motivated in some way, even if it is a motivation to do either as he is told, or please his wife there is something there to work with. If someone comes to you and asks for help you have a window of opportunity. Find what it is that motivated them to ask, give them the information they need and hope that something resonates. Quite often it did.

All this man needs is to have an open mind and listen.

Then there is the change we want for ourselves. Maybe a job, college course, house, partner, child; To be happy, fulfilled or at peace the list goes on.

Sometimes this can be easy but it can also be hard. There appears to be no rhyme or reason to this. Getting the job you want can take time. You may have to learn new skills, develop yourself, and network with the right people until it all falls into place.

Persistence is definitely important if you want something to change in your life. Maybe you want to meet someone. You need to keep scouring the dating sites, going out on dates, having an open mind and eventually you will meet someone you like enough to see again.

A client I worked with wanted to work as a chef in fine dining; he was struggling to find the right place for him. He spent time emailing and contacting suitable restaurants/kitchens, if they didn't have a position at that time he would offer himself for work experience, a week's unpaid work so they could get to know him. He did a few of these and eventually was offered the job he wanted. But all this took time, effort and money.

If you want to move, you spend time researching the area, what sort of house you want, calculating your budget and looking at lending options. All time consuming processes.

As a child when you learnt to walk, it took time, you kept trying, some of us longer than others. You fell a lot, it hurt, you cried. But eventually you walked.

There isn't a finite time limit on this. If you want to gain or remove something in your life you have to apply yourself and no one can guarantee how long this will take.

You might not need to change a lot to get to where you want to be but **there is no magic button!!!** No one can do it for you. You need to apply yourself if you want to change your habits, life, health, finances or more. Luckily it gets easier the more you do it. But you must keep going, if you want your life to be different, keep making changes until it works.

"YOUR LIFE DOES NOT GET
BETTER BY CHANCE,
IT GETS BETTER
WITH CHANGE."

Rachel's Story

Rachel suffered childhood abuse at the hands of her dad. As I am sure you can imagine the whole thing was incredibly painful and difficult for her and her mum. Rachel didn't want it to define her, she didn't want to become a victim or live her life like that. If you met Rachel you would have no way of knowing what happened to her. She has actively chosen for it to not be a part of who she is.

She actively sought out people she could learn from, so she could further her career but also learn about herself. She kept working at it and moved forward even though it was incredibly hard. She took part in some breakthrough coaching. This is an intensive process that looks at all areas of life and clears away negative emotions, enabling one to keep moving forward. She really wanted to let go of her past and was trying everything in her power to do this.

Rachel is a classic example of "I can learn anything, I can design my life and how do I want to be." And this isn't things on the outside like what car I want to drive or where I want to live. It was what sort of person she wanted to be and how she wants to feel in her day-to-day life.

Now, it wasn't easy, she worked at it. She asked for help and kept going every day.

More than anything she wanted to be in a relationship and get married. This was very scary for her as her most important male relationship with her father had seriously let her down.

Logically she knew that not all men were the same but it didn't stop the emotion and how she felt about this.

She met someone and fell in love, he was very understanding about her situation and did everything he could to support her. We worked together on her relationship, commitment issues, which were ultimately about fear from her childhood. She had a lovely wedding day, everything she and her partner dreamed of and they have been very happily married now for over 5 years.

I watched her grow and change from a young woman who had an idea of how she wanted her life to be, to becoming that woman, living her life by design. Not just living it from outside. She felt good, it wasn't a struggle. I am not saying it was plain sailing. But she continued to keep going, growing, learning and changing; because she wanted to and because she believed it was possible. She was the designer of her life.

5. What are the most important things to know when stopping your bad habits?

There are many bad habits we might struggle with at any given time. Maybe when we started it wasn't such a bad thing. Take smoking for instance. Depending on how old you are you might remember a time when it was ok to smoke. Go back far enough and we were actively encouraged to smoke with posters extoling the virtues of tobacco. I know, hard to believe but true. When I started smoking in the early 80's it was just the done thing, it wasn't until a bit later that we all became aware of the health risks. By then I definitely had a bad habit.

It is the same with alcohol. It's only very recently that there is some great public health information out there. However, we still have that strange thing like we did with tobacco where big advertising companies are creating amazing adverts selling us a lifestyle depending on what we choose to drink. Alcohol advertising is big business just like tobacco used to be. I have even seen some health adverts claiming that alcohol reduces the onset of dementia or to drink red wine because of the anti-oxidants. I think it's fair to say as a population we are undecided about whether alcohol is a good habit or bad. The messages we receive are ambivalent let's face it. Very clear public health messages everywhere telling us to be careful and why, then all those lovely shiny lifestyle alcohol adverts selling us a dream, it's no wonder we are confused.

Ok so forget all of that, forget the lifestyle adverts, forget the friend that can drink and still look good without any problems, forget the TV programs that have people clearly drinking buckets of wine and they still get up in the morning looking great. It's not real and it's not you!

What I want you to do is to think about the reason you are reading this book and how it affects you.

Does it cause you a problem? Is drinking an issue for you?

The **good news is you weren't born doing it, you have learnt it and if you have learnt it you can UN learn it!!**

What is a Habit?

What is a habit anyway? It's a recurrent, often unconscious pattern of behaviour that is acquired through frequent repetition: such as having to get up early for a short period of time but then after a few weeks you wake up early anyway. Or going to the gym because you need to lose weight, get healthier or fitter. Initially it's a struggle and you have to force yourself to go. However, after a few weeks you look forward to it (well sometimes, maybe that's going a bit too far), your body needs to exercise and you notice how good you feel afterwards.

Just checking you got that bit**? It's a recurrent, often unconscious pattern of behaviour that is acquired through frequent repetition**. (Keep going, persist).

Our habits are with us where ever we go – they are our constant companion.

Our habits can be our greatest helper or one of your heaviest burdens. When you manage to master a good habit, it feels great and can really make a difference to your life. Such as drinking less when you go out, initially it might feel different, but if you stick to it, week by week it becomes easier to say no, to drink soft drinks or maybe even do something different. Especially as you start to feel the benefits.

A habit can drive us forward to live the life we want or it can drag us down to failure. When we are really focussed and have a plan it can feel great and our good habits can really help to move us along in life. If you are allowing your bad habits to affect your life, it's time you took charge of them.

The thing that most people don't realise though is that we are in charge of our habits – with some practice that is. You are in the driving seat of the habit control centre.

Habits are easily managed, you just need to be firm initially to get the habit in there – don't give up be persistent. (There it is again ☺)

So, are you at cause or effect?

Do things just happen to you and you are unsure why?

Or are you in charge?

Take the habit, train yourself, be strong, be persistent, don't give up and before you know it will become ingrained and you won't have to think about it so much.

How Do You know if your drinking is an issue?

Ask yourself these questions.

Do you think about alcohol every day?

Do you do it every day?

If I said take 7 days off, how would you feel, could you do it, now?

When was the last time you had 7 days off?

Are you tired?

Do you feel unhealthy?

Do you feel unfulfilled, you know there are other things you want to be doing?

Do you feel guilt and shame because of your drinking?

Is it causing problems in your relationships?

Is it causing problems at work?

Is it causing problems financially?

If you answered yes to any of these questions it would be a good idea to take a break.

Be clear about what the problem is.

If you are doing something daily that is causing a problem for you then surely you would like to change it so it's not a problem?

If you can't go a week without doing it, you need to spend some time learning how to change this, so you break the habit, the pattern.

If it's causing a problem somewhere for you, be honest, how would it improve your life if you made some changes?

Practice

Until it becomes
A good habit.

6. Alcohol

If any of what I have said so far resonates with you I highly recommend you take a break from your drinking. Even if it's just for 30 days. I mean 30 days is nothing, right?

Whether you think so or not alcohol will be a factor in whatever it is that is going wrong in your life. And like Jane, before it's good to clear it out of the way and see what else is going on.

It's hard to change and improve your life if you are drinking. Think about it in terms of taking some time off to really focus on you.

Depending on how you drink will depend on whether you need to reduce slowly or if you can just stop. This is really important with alcohol.

There are many benefits to taking a break or reducing your intake.

No more wasted time on hangovers, feeling rubbish, worrying about what you did the night before, saying the wrong thing, making mistakes that put everyone at risk, damaging your health or maybe even your pocket. No more weight gain, the list goes on and on.

People who live happy healthy lives generally don't drink that much. I know there is always the exception. But I would even challenge that, as what can appear a happy healthy life on the outside can be fraught with difficulties on the inside. Plus there are the health risks to consider.

For instance, I know a man that has drunk all his life pretty much nearly every day. He has taken the odd 3 months off here and there (and felt really good). Sometimes he only drinks 2/3 cans of lager, however sometimes he drinks more up to 10 cans. From the outside looking in he has a happy healthy life, he would also say this if asked. However, he has a big belly (that's definitely the drink) he also suffers with over acidity – again alcohol is a contributing factor. His wife is worried and unhappy. She would prefer it if he didn't drink or just drink occasionally. She loves him and is concerned for his health and their future. What would she do if he died first? Finances are also a concern as he needs to drive for work. Because she is worried she brings it up quite often and it causes regular arguments.

On the outside it looks like his drinking isn't impacting on his life, but look deeper and it does cause problems.

I am not selling a miracle but ask anyone that has taken a break or stopped for a while and they will tell you how good they felt and how it has improved all areas of their life.

In 11 years no one has ever come back to me and told me their life got worse after taking a break from drinking.

Getting a Measure on your Drinking

The first thing we need to do is find out how much you are drinking. This is really important to know. Once we have that we can find out what it means for you.

How do you figure out how much you are drinking and how much is too much?

We are told that the recommended guidelines for alcohol are around 2-3 units, however it's good if people can have at least 2 alcohol free days. It's really important that you don't drink everyday – this is how some people get into trouble, building up a habit.

See below an example of a drink diary.

Day	What/how much	time	Where/who with	totals
Mon	2 glasses of 175ml red wine	6pm start Until 9pm	At home While cooking dinner and doing chores	5 units 318 calories £3.50

Tues	2 glasses of 175ml red wine	6pm start Until 9pm	At home While cooking dinner. Helping kids with homework	5 units 318 calories £3.50
Wed	2 glasses of 175ml red wine	5pm – 7pm	meet a colleague after work, in a bar in town.	5 units 318 calories £8.00
Thurs	1 Gin and tonic Self-pour	7pm	At home	3 units 250 calories £1.50
Friday	1 bttle of wine	6pm	Out with friends for dinner	9 units 700 calories £15.00
Sat	1bttle of wine 2 cocktails	7pm	Friends birthday party	9 units + 6 units 1300 calories £25.00
Sunday	No alcohol as felt a bit rough			
			Total	42 units 3204 calories £56.50

So, what is a unit and how do you measure them. This depends on how you drink your alcohol; there are several ways to do this:

2-3 units look like 3 x 25ml shots of a spirit such as vodka/gin/whisky. Basically a 25ml shot of a spirit 40% ABV is 1 unit.

1 pint of 4% beer is about 2.2 units.

A medium sized glass 175ml of wine is 2.3 units.

A standard bottle of wine is about 9 units.

Have a look on the drink aware website or any reputable health website that will give a unit calculator, this is the easiest way to do this.

Even though units are annoying, don't make sense to anyone and are hard to figure out. They do actually work in terms of figuring out how much you are drinking and helps with cutting back. Trust me.

This is the formula for working units out if you are interested Multiply the total volume of a drink (in ml) by its ABV (measured as a percentage) and dividing the result by 1,000.

For example, **to work out** the number of **units** in a pint (568ml) of strong lager (ABV 5.2%): 5.2 (%) x 568 (ml) ÷ 1,000 = 2.95 **units**.

Task

Let's look at last week. For every day write down what you drank, what time you started, and how much. But be honest. Make sure you understand the size of your drinks.

If you are drinking and self-pouring at home the first thing to do is get a unit measurer. People who drink at home and self-pour tend to drink more.

When you have a week's drinking written down, go onto any website or good app with a unit calculator. Make a note of your units for each day then your total for the week. There are also some apps out there so you can calculate your units as you drink.

If you aren't a regular drinker but a binge drinker you may want to look at how much you drank the last time you drank a lot. By binge I mean a man who drinks more than 8 units in a single session or a woman more than 6, so for instance 8 units could be 4 x pints or just under a bottle of wine, a lady 3 glasses of wine or 6 single gins. So a binge isn't that much really.

Don't worry the more you keep a track of your drinking, the easier it becomes to measure your units and keep track.

I can be out with friends and can calculate everyone's units for the night. As I am sure you can tell, I am not popular on a night out. I don't volunteer the information obviously, it's only if they ask.

By now you should have a measure of the level of your drinking, however if you are reading this I am guessing your drinking is causing you some problems already or maybe you are just curious.

Physical Dependency

If you are drinking a large amount daily and you have a physical dependency then you must consult with a medical professional prior to reducing. This may also be the case if you drink large amounts in one go say over 60 units in a binge drinking session – over a couple of days that is.

Physical and psychological dependency is very important where alcohol is concerned, there are very few drugs (yes, I am calling alcohol a drug because that is what it is) that are physically and psychologically addictive.

So what does it mean to be physically addicted? If you drink a large amount of alcohol daily or a large amount in a binge session and you stopped suddenly you would go into a physical withdrawal.

Symptoms of alcohol withdrawal are:

- Sweating.
- Shaking
- Nausea
- Anxiety

- Paranoia
- Insomnia
- In severe cases: whole body shakes, fits and hallucinations.

Alcohol withdrawal can be fatal. If you think you are physically dependant, please go and see a medical professional before embarking on any reduction. As tempting as it is to just stop when you have really had enough I strongly advise you seek medical help. It's not worth the risk.

This only effects a small number of people. So, if you are drinking large amounts daily, or big binge sessions and you experience any of the above symptoms please get help.

Alcohol and your emotional health.

Alcohol is a depressant drug so I have met many people who are drinking and are struggling with anxiety and depression either separately or both. Many people, once they have sorted their drinking out, feel a lot better emotionally and physically. There are a few people who are drinking to manage their anxiety and depression which has usually been there prior to the drink problems. (If this is the case for you again please seek medical help.)

Remember: If you are concerned see your doctor.

How Does Alcohol Effect Your Body and Brain?

- Alcohol acts as a depressant on the brain and initially you can feel relaxed and happy then it can make you feel depressed and low afterwards. In the long term it can kill brain cells and lead to memory loss.

- Too much alcohol can dehydrate the body which is bad news for your skin. It also dilates the blood vessels which can lead to veins on the face. Alcohol is not a good look in many ways. So, from a pure vanity perspective it's great to take a break from alcohol. It makes me laugh reading all those women's mags talking about beauty products, particularly skin products. When one thing most women and men can do straight away to improve their skin is take time off from the alcohol and drink more water. You don't need to buy an expensive cream.

- Alcohol can blur vision which makes it harder to judge speed and distances.

- It can affect your sleep. Too much alcohol effects REM sleep which is the most important part. Your body needs deep sleep to repair itself.

- Alcohol relaxes you and when we drink too much it lowers our inhibitions causing us to do things we wouldn't normally do: get over emotional, have arguments, fights, have accidents and make silly mistakes that can cause big problems for our life.

- Drinking large amounts of alcohol over short periods of time can cause irregular heartbeat and shortness of breath.
- Alcohol is absorbed from the stomach into the blood stream. Your ability to break down alcohol depends on many things including age, weight and sex. On average your body breaks down 1 unit per hour, drinking more than that will build up your blood alcohol concentration and if you drink a lot in one night it may be many hours before you are alcohol free. This is another reason we talk about units so much and teach people what they are and how to count them. It really helps you to manage whether you still have alcohol in your system.
- Drinking too much in one go or even over regular periods can affect your performance in the bedroom. If you have drunk a lot your inhibitions will be lowered and you may have unsafe sex or have sex you later regret.
- Alcohol is very calorific and can cause you to put on weight. Or maybe you are skipping meals so you can drink. Alcohol is empty calories, it has no nutritional value. On a night out it also increases your appetite.
- Liver breaks down most of the alcohol a person drinks, however it can only break down 1 unit per hour, more than that and the liver struggles to cope, if someone drinks a huge amount in one go a person can fall into an alcoholic coma and it can be fatal, alcohol poisoning. Long term drinking causes liver disease and liver cancer;

it's called the silent disease as symptoms aren't noticeable until its fairly advanced.

- Just to make sure you got that, if you drink too much alcohol in one go you can die. Its not an exact amount and the amount is different for each person.

This is just a taster of the health risks in drinking more than the recommended guidelines. Alcohol literally effects every part of the body. It increases our risk of cancers, strokes, diabetes.

A Deeper Look

Everyone is effected differently by the issues drinking alcohol causes. Different issues may cause more of a problem for some than others. You know your body and your mind. For some people it will be the binge that's the problem, so the health risks but also the problems that happen on a night out. For other's it will be little things like, sleep, stress, anxiety, weight, stomach problems or it just generally getting in the way of life.

Imagine what you could do with your life if you weren't drinking? How much more time, energy you would have, maybe even money.

If you are really interested in the health risks and want to find out more (I strongly advise you do).

Check out https://www.drinkaware.co.uk/alcohol-facts/health-effects-of-alcohol/ for more information.

Some Facts and Figures About Alcohol in the UK

Alcohol Concern has said the health service was facing an "intolerable strain" from people drinking too much.

The statistics also highlight how hospital casualty departments are now being swamped with people with alcohol related problems.

The figures released by the charity showed the number of booze-related NHS admissions, including hospital patients and clinic and A&E visits reached **9.9 million** in England in 2012-13.

This is compared to 1.2 million alcohol-related hospital admissions in England in 2011-12, when the figures did not include outpatient admissions and A&E trips, Alcohol Concern said.

Some 9.6 million people are now drinking in excess of Government guidelines - including 2.4 million who are classed as "high risk", according to the charity.

High risk drinking is defined as people who drink more than six to eight units of alcohol a day, with one unit equating to less than a small glass of wine or a half pint of beer.

According to Alcohol Concern, men aged 55-75 were the most likely to be admitted to hospital due to alcohol misuse.

It revealed almost half of all head and neck cancer patient admissions were alcohol-related (47.4%), costing the NHS £65.3 million.

Just over 13% of all malignant tumours of breast cancer patients were also attributed to alcohol, at a cost of £27.1 million to the NHS, Alcohol Concern said.

While A&E admissions accounted for 6 in 10 alcohol-related hospital visits, inpatient admissions were responsible for almost two thirds of the total cost burden of £2.8 billion, according to the charity.

The South East of England was revealed as the region with the most "high risk" drinkers, with more than 1.6 million people. While the North West had the most alcohol-related deaths with 3,501 in 2012.

http://www.alcoholconcern.org.uk/campaign/alcohol-harm-map Information from Alcohol concern.

All of this may sound that I am scare-mongering and I am one of those people who doesn't want anyone to have any fun. Trust me I want you to have fun and be happy. I just don't want you to die whilst doing it. I haven't lifted this information for the hell of it. I ran a very successful alcohol treatment service for 4 years. This is all true, people are dying, they are ill and this isn't just street drinkers. Alcohol doesn't discriminate, it's everyone and anyone, it really is. Young and old, poor and rich, successful and unemployed. It is a mix of people who drink and get into to trouble with it. It also never ceases to amaze me how badly informed these people where. There were very few people we spoke to that actually knew what the health risks where. There appears to be some silly illusion that because it is legal and there are all those lovely glossy adverts it must be ok. Coupled with the way our media reports on drug related deaths and anything drug related, I can sort of understand how that might happen. Alcohol is one of our most harmful substances, it's up there with heroin and cocaine, in the top 3. If they were reclassifying all drugs (including alcohol) today alcohol would be a class A illegal drug.

I am still flabbergasted that yes, I can go to my corner shop and buy a bottle of vodka for £10 and potentially kill myself.

Whilst the media reports on young people dying at festivals from taking recreational drugs, who's deaths could have been prevented, by good education and testing at clubs and festivals.

No amount of testing will change the fact that alcohol is a poison and taken in large amounts in one go can kill you, as well as taken regularly in significant amounts over a period of time will also make you very ill and potentially kill you.

And this is why I go on and on about alcohol.

What You Can Do

The most important thing, once you know that you want to make a change and why, is what you can do about it?

Sometimes learning about alcohol and making a record of how much you are drinking can be enough for some people. Most people don't know how much they are drinking. I can remember the first time I learnt about units and calculated how much I had drunk one weekend I was horrified. By this point I had already stopped as I had hit my rock bottom. It was just another piece of information that added to my motivation.

But if that isn't enough for you here are some options to reduce safely:

- Delay your start time: If when you finish work the first thing you do is have a drink, don't, do something different. Have a cup of tea, go to the gym, go for a walk, do an evening class, play a game with the kids, visit a friend that doesn't drink or go and watch a film. The ideas are endless.
- Swap your wine/beer for a lower % so you are drinking the same amount but less alcohol.
- Slowly reduce the amount you drink: Start with ¾ of a bottle for a week, then go to 1/2 a bottle, then have an alcohol-free day. This will be when you really need to do something different.

- Measure out your drinks: Make sure you are only drinking your spirits one unit at a time with a lot of mixer.
- Have a soft drink first: If you drink out this is really important. Whether you realise it or not most people when they go out, particularly on a binge get excited. They drink their first drink quickly and then continue, this is how people get drunk very quickly. When you get to 3 or 4 drinks it's hard to stop. (Now I am generalising, however it's like this for a lot of people.)
- Drink soft drinks in between alcohol drinks: If you are on a night out with friends doing this will mean you will watch your friends get drunk a lot quicker than you. This will also help you to slow down as it's not a great look being drunk. (I realise this is a very selfish point of view, watching your friends get drunk is not a responsible grown up thing to advise, however we are talking about you. Whatever it takes to help you stay motivated. Once you have it cemented then it will help the people around you).
- Drink drinks with a lot of mixers in: Not only does this reduce the amount of alcohol you are drinking; it also changes the taste. We want to tackle habits in lots of different ways. A lot of people tell me they love the way red wine, whiskies, ale and gin etc. tastes. But if you are one of these people you have become accustomed to the taste. Quite frankly if you are not used to it alcohol tastes awful. Remember the first time you tried alcohol,

it was probably disgusting and you couldn't figure out why people were drinking it. Maybe you even had to train yourself to drink it and get used to the taste. But the good news is, you guessed it. If you can train yourself to like the taste, then you can train yourself to unlike it. Drinking soft drinks, adding lots of mixer will start this process. Keep going even if you don't like it at first. If it continues to be a real problem, then change your drink.

- Focus on your goals: What can happen is people challenge and push you to drink alcoholic drinks, even grown adults and good friends. It never ceases to amaze me how badly behaved grown, responsible intelligent people can be when we are out drinking. I have done it myself. Be ready for this, be prepared. You can always buy your own, just say you are not doing rounds tonight, then you can buy drinks that could be alcoholic – no one will know or question. Lemonade could be G & T, a coke could be anything. Be really clear about what you are doing and why. People tend to accept, a break for charity, training for an event, allergies, medication, driving etc. It's up to you, just feel good about what you are saying.

- The Takeaway Rule: Think of alcohol in the same way you think of a takeaway (I am assuming you don't have takeaway every night?). We have already found out that alcohol has nothing in it of any use to you what so ever, in fact it's a toxin, a poison. It depends on the type of takeaway you get but mostly they are not that good for you. Usually high in fat, sugar etc. and probably a day's calories in one hit. So, would you eat a takeaway every night? Generally a takeaway is a treat or a reward that you have occasionally, you recognise it's not good for you. So if alcohol actually is worse for you in terms of nutritional value, why are you having it every night?

- Eat regularly and healthily: What you eat can have a large impact on your mood. Having an unhealthy diet and irregular eating patterns can make you anxious, irritable and depressed which can make you more likely to drink. Eating well makes you feel good and makes it much easier to cultivate a new habit. Eating healthy food can also help your body to repair the damage caused by your drinking.

- Drink lower % drinks: If you are a prosecco/champagne drinker, Buck's fizz is great and only 3 units a bottle.

- Throw alcohol away that you don't drink: This is very powerful. Do it.

- Buy the smaller bottles. If you buy a normal bottle of wine and you are reducing it can be hard, there it is in the fridge talking to you. Also there is that old fashioned British thing about not throwing things away. Start as you mean to go on, buy the smaller bottles and then that's it, reduction done.

- Take a break: Maybe 30 days, 60 or 90 days. Just to see how you feel and if it improves your life? If you need to and it helps, do challenges. I run a very supportive

Facebook group for Women who want to change their relationship with alcohol. There is Stoptober, Dry January, challenges for charity, Weight Watchers, Slimming World etc.

- Follow a programme: Something like the Stop drinking and start living online coaching programme I run in my group. Anything like this gives you structure, something to focus on.
  The point is you learn things about yourself and how to look after yourself.

- Join a group: There are SMART groups and AA groups if that is the sort of thing that helps and many internet forums as well.

- Read books about the subject, memoirs etc: There are many out there to educate you even further.

This isn't an extensive list. What works for one person will not for another. Start by trying a few until you find what works for you. My experience is that you try everything and you keep trying and some of it works. That you build a box of tools.

Binge drinkers

If you don't drink regularly but when you do, you drink too much. Start with making a note of how much you drink on a night out and calculate your units. Sometimes this can be enough. I remember the first time I was taught this and I was horrified at the amount I had drunk over a weekend, also in the class I was in the teacher made an example of me because of the amount I had drunk (any trainers or workers out there do not ever do this) by the time he had finished with me I wanted to go and have a drink!

This is where an app can be really good, something that will track your units and maybe even calories, money spent?

Think about all the things you can do to change your night out as we have talked about. Make a list and try them 1 by 1, keep going until you have a strategy that works

Binges can be really dangerous. All it takes is for you to be in the wrong place at the wrong time, a little bit too drunk and things can go horribly wrong. I have known many people that this has happened to, some people have been lucky and used it as a wakeup call. However, others haven't been so lucky.

Once you have calculated the amount you consume on a binge, it maybe useful to make a list of the possible things that could go wrong while you are intoxicated. When you are drunk, you are very vulnerable, anything can happen, it really is wrong place, wrong time. This goes for men as well, even big men. Fights can go horribly wrong when people have been drinking.

Quite often those fights wouldn't have happened if drink wasn't involved.

Follow the advice and tips in the What can you do section. Particularly the have a soft drink first one. Then you can relax and settle into your evening, slowly. Remember it's the getting excited, nervous, drinking quickly and too much in one go that is the issue here. Slow down, there is no rush, the slower you drink, the more soft drinks you have, the better you will feel. Logging your drinks into an app as you go along can really help to, to see how much you are drinking, calories and money spent can be really motivating.

Binge Drinker and when things go wrong.

Kerry was in her 30's had 2 children and a partner she loved. Life was good, yes, she was tired, yes kids, work and relationship all took its toll, but she knew she had it good. Every now and then she loved to go out and party, in her younger days at university she had been a bit of a party animal and there was a small part of her that missed that life. So when it was a friends birthday it was a great excuse for everyone to get together and have some fun.

Because she didn't go out very often, or drink regularly, she had no tolerance. She would also be very excited, all the friends would be. All that collective excitement together, everyone getting together and drinking. She drank quite a bit in a short period of time and was quite drunk, they went on to a club.

She got talking to an old boyfriend and he offered her some cocaine. Because she was drunk she said yes and had a few lines. She hasn't taken any drugs apart from alcohol since she was in her early 20's. Because they where getting on so well and helped along with the alcohol and cocaine, they got caught up in the moment and ended up going back to his place. She spent the night with him, they had unprotected sex.

In the morning she was mortified, very hungover and struggling with guilt and shame. Her friends where really worried about her as well as she had just disappeared.

She went home to her family. However then having to deal with the fact that she had been unfaithful to her partner, putting everything that was important to her at risk.

She had to go to the doctors and get a morning after pill and book into the sexual health clinic for tests.

This is the first time she had done anything like this in a relationship. If she hadn't drunk so much, been so under the influence, she wouldn't have taken the cocaine or gone home with the old boyfriend.

Summary

- If you drink regularly in large amounts you will build up a physical addiction and may need a medically assisted detox.
- Keep a diary.
- Count your units (count your calories if this helps you to stay motivated).
- Delay your start time.
- Alcohol free days. This is a must so as not to build up bad habits.
- Mess with your habits and patterns: This one is really important. Change the taste, the times you drink, what can you do instead of drinking. Etc.
- Eat well.
- Drink soft drinks.
- Drink lower % drinks.
- Throw alcohol away if you don't drink it.
- Buy smaller bottles.
- Take a break. Make sure you have big gaps of time, spaces, when you don't drink. One month, 3 months even longer if you can.
- The takeaway rule.
- Do challenges to help motivate.
- Follow a programme.
- Join a group.

Keep learning and trying new things. Build up a list of resources and tips that work for you, even if they work for a short time then keep coming back to them. Its like having a tool box.

7. Food

We need to talk about food. I know this is essentially about alcohol, however a lot of people get out of the habit of eating properly. Eating well, eating whole foods, real food, will help you to feel better emotionally and physically. Its also about putting new good habits in.

Eating unhealthy food, whether takeaways, junk food or sugar is a curse of our generation. We have access to pretty much everything we could ever think of and more. It's on every corner of every street. There are reminders of it at every glance, in our newsfeeds on social media, TV and films. We have never had it so good or bad depending on your perspective. Similar to alcohol when something is readily available it can be really hard to control or manage your cravings and desires.

Maybe you are eating badly while drinking, or maybe when you stop drinking your eating becomes an issue. Sometimes people replace the alcohol with sugar. Initially I say work on the alcohol, focus on that, however have an eye to this. Sugar intake can easily turn into your next issue. Thinking about what you can eat, what is good for you will help. Rather than focusing more on what you can't have.

When I talk about food, I am talking about eating whole foods, real foods, variety, eating for health, not diets. That's really important. Diets don't work because they focus on what you can't have. Whereas if you focus on eating for health, what you an eat, what is good for you, life is easier.

I just want to give you a bit of an overview about junk food. Here are the facts and figures (excuse the pun). You know I love starting with the facts, because well there is so much mis information out there.

The Effect of Junk Food on Your Body

One in four British adults are obese, according to the UN Food and Agriculture Organisation. Prompting fears that the UK has become the "fat man of Europe".

The UK has the highest level of obesity in Western Europe, ahead of countries such as France, Germany, Spain and Sweden, the 2013 report says.

Obesity levels in the UK have more than trebled in the last 30 years and, on current estimates, more than half the population could be obese by 2050.
Europe's obesity league:

- UK: 24.9%
- Ireland: 24.5%
- Spain: 24.1%
- Portugal: 21.6%

- Germany: 21.3%
- Belgium: 19.1%
- Austria: 18.3%
- Italy: 17.2%
- Sweden: 16.6%
- France: 15.6%

Source: The State of Food and Agriculture 2013 (PDF, 2.44Mb), United Nations Food and Agricultural Organization.

"The UK is the 'fat man' of Europe," writes Professor Terence Stephenson in Measuring Up, a report on the nation's obesity crisis by the Academy of Medical Royal Colleges (AoMRC). "It is no exaggeration to say that it is the biggest public health crisis facing the UK today," he says.

The consequences of obesity on our health include diabetes, heart disease cancer, and people dying needlessly from avoidable diseases.
Britain has become an "an obese society" where being overweight is "normal". It is a trend three decades in the making which, according to experts, will take several more to reverse.

What is Obese?

A person is considered overweight if they have a body mass index (BMI) between 25 and 29, and obese with a BMI of 30 and above.

In England, 24.8% of adults are obese and 61.7% are either overweight or obese, according to the Health and Social Care Information Centre. Today's obesity levels are more than three times what they were in 1980, when only 6% of men and 8% of women were obese.

How Has the Obesity Crisis Happened?

Recent research has challenged the idea that obesity is simply the result of the individual "eating too much and doing too little".

Rising obesity is not the result of a national collapse in willpower. Studies have shown the environment has a major influence on the decisions people make about their lifestyle. Known as "obesogenic environments", these are places, often urban, that encourage unhealthy eating and inactivity.

The cause of the rapid rise in obesity has been blamed on our modern lifestyles, including our reliance on the car, TVs, computers, desk-bound jobs and high-calorie food.

The car, TV, computers, desk jobs, high-calorie food, and clever food marketing have all contributed to encourage inactivity and overeating. "Obesity is a consequence of the abundance and convenience of modern life as well as the human body's propensity to store fat," says Professor Jebb. Research has shown that we have a natural tendency to store fat – it's a survival mechanism that helped early humans survive famine and food shortages. "The situation in which food is readily available for most people has arrived in a blink of an eye in evolutionary terms," says Jebb.

Adults spend about six hours a day engaged in sedentary pursuits (watching TV and other screen time, reading and other low-energy activities). On average, men and women spend 2.8 hours watching television per weekday and this rises to about three hours on weekends.

The average distance a person walked for transport purposes has fallen from 255 miles a year in 1976 to 192 miles in 2003, while car use increased by more than 10%. Although people are travelling further to get to work, one in five journeys of less than one mile are made by car. "Your likelihood of being active is shaped by the environment you live in," says Professor Jebb. "For example, you're more likely to ride a bike if there are safe and convenient cycle lanes."

In 2012, only 67% of men and 55% of women aged 16 and over met the government's recommendations for physical activity of 150 minutes a week. Among children aged 5 to 15, more boys (21%) than girls (16%) met the recommendation to do an hour of activity every day.

Leisure time is increasingly spent indoors whereas the incentives for outdoor play have fallen due to safety concerns and a lack of access to green spaces or sports facilities. Longer working hours and more desk-bound jobs over the past decades have resulted in limiting opportunities for other forms of activity during the working day.

Breastfeeding, healthy weaning practices and the mother's own diet have all been linked to reduced obesity later in life although why this is the case has yet to be fully explained.

What's the Big Deal with Obesity?
Being overweight or obese increases the risk of many serious illnesses, such as type 2 diabetes, high blood pressure, heart disease, stroke, as well as cancer. "People are dying needlessly from avoidable diseases," wrote Prof Stephenson in the AoMRC's Measuring Up report.

Compared with a healthy weight man, an obese man is:
- Five times more likely to develop type 2 diabetes.

- Three times more likely to develop cancer of the colon.
- More than two and a half times more likely to develop high blood pressure – a major risk factor for stroke and heart disease.

An obese woman, compared with a healthy weight woman, is:
- almost 13 times more likely to develop type 2 diabetes.
- more than four times more likely to develop high blood pressure.
- more than three times more likely to have a heart attack.

People from some ethnic groups, including south Asians, who are more likely to be overweight and obese, also have a higher risk of type 2 diabetes and other weight-related illnesses.

A BMI of 30 to 35 has been found to reduce life expectancy by an average of three years, while a BMI of over 40 reduced longevity by eight to 10 years, which is equivalent to a lifetime of smoking. "As a society, we are gradually realising that obesity poses just as serious a health threat as smoking," says Dr Tedstone.

Obesity has been blamed for about 30,000 deaths a year in the UK, 9,000 of those taking place before retirement age. Alongside disease, obesity can affect peoples' ability to get and hold down work, their self-esteem, their wellbeing and mental health.

What Are We Doing About it?

Reversing the obesity trend will require society as a whole to think differently. For government and businesses, it means creating an environment that encourages healthier eating and physical activity. **For individuals and families, it means eating better quality foods and moving more.**
It will require a major shift in thinking, not just by government, but by individuals, families, business and society in general.

Currently, no country in the world has a comprehensive, long-term strategy to deal with the challenges posed by obesity. The only country to have successfully reversed its obesity problem was Cuba, although it was the unexpected consequence of an economic downturn in the early 1990s. This caused severe food and fuel shortages, which resulted in an average weight loss per citizen of 5.5kg over the course of the five-year economic crisis. During this time there was a significant drop in prevalence of, and deaths due to, cardiovascular diseases, type 2 diabetes and cancers. A study based on the Cuban experience concludes that national initiatives encouraging people to eat less and exercise more could be effective at tackling obesity levels.

The UK government has recognised that past efforts have not succeeded in turning the tide and that a new approach is required. In 2011, it published <u>Healthy Lives, Healthy People (PDF, 575kb)</u>, a policy document setting out its vision for how society as a whole can work together to turn the tide on obesity by 2020.

Some of the UK's government's measures to help people make healthier choices include:

- Giving people advice on healthier food choices and physical activity through the <u>Change4Life</u> programme.
- Improving labelling on food and drink to help people make healthy choices.
- Encouraging businesses on the high street to include calorie information on their menus so people can make healthy choices.
- Giving people guidance on how much physical activity they should be doing.

The UK government has also asked businesses to play their part in helping everyone, from staff to customers, make healthier choices through its Responsibility Deal pledges.
Food manufacturers, retailers and the hospitality sector have committed to cutting down on the amount of fat, sugar and salt in popular food products encouraging people to eat more fruit

and vegetables, reducing portion sizes and putting calorie information on menus.

Each of us is ultimately responsible for our own health. We should be free to make choices about diet and physical activity for ourselves and for our families. "However, supermarkets and food manufacturers are already making choices for us by deciding how much fat and sugar to put in their products and what items to stock and promote," says Professor Jebb. "Government can play a positive role in working with the private sector to help people make healthier choices to prevent weight gain." Given all the external causes of the obesity epidemic, for the individual, it boils down to the simple message: to lose weight, you need to eat less and move more. "People don't choose to be obese," says Professor Jebb. "It just happens for a number of reasons. We should stop blaming people for being fat and instead support them in controlling their weight. "We've all got the potential to be fat. In the environment we live in, it's easy to overeat and be less active. Some people need to work harder than others at keeping weight gain in check."

Taken from

So, things have changed a lot and we need to catch up and adjust in the right way. Not feeling bad and eating on our couch. Remember this "**We need to move more and eat good quality foods**" it really is that simple, I would also add eat wholefoods, real foods. You don't need a fancy diet, actually its been proved that diets don't work.

So yes there are issues with the way the world has changed however we are in charge of us, what we eat, how we exercise, how we live. Same as reducing drinking, we can also eat healthy foods and exercise.

What You Can Do

Before we get into this there are some questions I would like you to ask yourself?

- Do you eat sugary and junk foods every day?
- Can you live without it?
- Can you go a week without having some sugar or junk food? (Just to be clear sugary things cakes, sweets, biscuits, puddings, junk food, crisps, takeaway food with no nutritional value)
- Do you find yourself eating more and more rubbish? (Let's be honest here the more we have the more we want).
- Do you feel bad? Do you give yourself a hard time after you have eaten too much rubbish?
- Are you overweight because of your bad eating habits?

- Does your health suffer?
- Once you start eating do you find it hard to stop?

If you answered yes to any of these questions it is worth you changing your focus with your eating habits.

I think the most important point here is when we eat a mostly healthy diet, so whole foods, real foods, we feel better. When we stop drinking we feel better, healthier, happier. Eating 3 good healthy meals a day will do this as well and exercising. Simple things we need to do better that will significantly improve our life.

I haven't just made this up either, I have seen it in all my work over the last 11 years, even with people with Mental health problems. Getting the basics in place is only going to improve your life.

What are the most important things you need to know?

The first thing you need to do is find out how much junk food you are eating. This is really important to know. How to reduce, cut back, get some control and be healthy. When are you eating, where and with whom?

It can be a powerful motivator to actually see what you are doing and helps to see if there any patterns. For instance, I used to really struggle during the afternoon, particularly in an office setting. So, time of day and environment is really important to me.

It's easier and more effective to do the diary as you go along in your week. Be honest, the only person you are cheating is yourself. Draw up a diary Monday to Sunday from the start of your day to the end. The first time I did this there wasn't enough space on the diary to write down everything I ate in one day. I am sure there are some great apps out there as well, let me know if you find a good one.

I have used My Fitness Pal, it tracks my calories, now I know that its not all about calories and calories don't really mean anything when it comes to health. However like units in alcohol, it is a way to measure amounts and monitor. It is one of the few things that helps me keep my eating in check. So it's a tool in my tool box that helps me to eat well and feel good.

Tracking can be really effective motivation to change your habits as some people don't realise how bad it is until it is written down in front of them.

Check for patterns in the positive and negative parts of the diary.

- Types of food: What kind of good and bad foods do you like?
- Times of the days: Are certain periods "danger" zones for you, whilst you find it easy to eat well in others.

- Certain people: Some may be a good influence on what you eat, some bad. As well as what junk is your favourite as we will all have some that we really struggle to resist.

Once you have identified patterns you can take action. If pizza is your kryptonite, just don't buy it, or even better learn how to make a homemade one. Replace it with something healthier.

When is the time of day you struggle most? Make sure you have a healthy alternative at the ready or even better change your day. For instance, if you struggle mid-afternoon, could you take a break then and have a hot drink, go for a walk or do something else you like doing that makes you feel good.

I have a couple of friends; they are both vegetarians. When I visit them the food is lovely, very healthy and nutritious,

I feel amazing when I have eaten with them, feels so good to eat healthy food and I don't crave anything rubbishy when I am with them. Because it isn't there, no temptation.

Maybe your partner is one of these annoying people that can eat and eat and eat and they bring you junk food as a treat. Explain to them how important this is to you and ask that they do other things for you to show they love you. Mostly people give you sugary junk food because they want to be nice, however it's not really. You can explain all of this to them. I am sure you can think of things they can do for you that are nice and good for your health.

Day	What/how much	time	Where/ who with	Totals Calories/ money
Mon	2 pieces of toast	8.00am	Home	250 calories
	Fruit	10.00am	Work	100
	Chicken salad wrap	12.00pm		400
	Chocolate biscuits x 2	2.00pm		150
	Chicken casserole and potatoes	6.00pm	home	500
	Rice pudding	8.00pm		300
Tues	Egg on toast	8.00am	Home	250 calories
	Croissant	10.00am	Work	350
	Soup and roll	1.00pm		450
	Cake	2.00pm		400
	Pie and chips	6.00pm	Home	800
	nuts	8.00pm		400
Wed	Cereal	7.00am	Home	
	Samosa	10.00am	Work	£1
	Sandwich, crisps	12.00pm		£4
	Fruit	2.00pm		£1
	Fizzy drink	3.00pm		£1
	Curry and rice	6.00pm	Out with friends	£15.00
Thur	Fruit and yoghurt	8.00am	Home	250 calories
	Kitkat	10.00am	Work	210
	Salad and fish	12.00pm		350
	Tea and Biscuits	2.00pm		150
	Sausage and Mash	7.00pm	Home	600
	Beer	7.00pm		130

Friday	Sausage sandwich	8.00am	Home	£4
	Coffee	9.00am	Meeting	£3
	Jacket potato with tuna	1.00pm		£5
	Nuts	3.00pm	At a	£1
	Pizza	7.00pm	friends	£12
	1bttle of wine			£10
Sat	Bacon, egg, sausage, hash brown, mushrooms etc	11.00am	Out with a friend	£8
	Beans on toast	5.00pm	Home	
	1 bttle of wine	8.00pm	pub	£10
	crisps			
Sun	Toast	10.00am	Home	
	Roast Dinner	2.00pm	Out with	£15
	Sandwich	6.00pm	family	
	2 x glasses of wine		home	£8
			Totals	

When you have a week's, eating written down find a calorie counter on the various sites on the web. Make a note of your calories for each day, then your total for the week. There are also some apps out there so you can calculate your calories as you eat if you want. Now I don't want you to get too caught up on calories as it's not about this. Calories don't actually mean anything in terms of health. It's about eating real food and breaking bad habits ultimately – giving you some control. However, I have noticed over the years that calories can really motivate people, giving them that initial boost. It might also help to make a note of how much the items cost. Especially if you are someone that eats out a lot. This is really important. What I am giving you information on is a number of different ways you can motivate yourself. Try all of them and find the ones that work for you. When one of these tips really helps you use it. Don't worry if you don't know a lot about food. A simple rule to follow is eat foods in their natural form. No processed foods. Ask yourself is this real food? **Eating real food is way more important for your health than counting calories.**

Remember diets don't work, they don't work because you eat a certain way for a certain period of time and then you go back to your eating habits before. Or the eating plan/diet was unrealistic. Its better to focus on eating for health and lifestyle as a long term plan.

Celebration and Reward

I remember as a child we just didn't eat junk food very often, everything was cooked from scratch, no ready meals. Very rarely did we ever go out for dinner it just wasn't on our radar. However when we did have something, sweets, crisps, chips etc. it was a treat. Particularly in the UK historically, when raising our children there has been a mentality that sweet things, rubbishy things are treats. I think it goes back to the war when things where rationed, so things like cake where a treat. The children that grew up in that way, are our parents, so it has continued even though, we are now living in a ridiculously abundant food society in the western world. So we have learnt this very early on. After all it's nice to treat ourselves. I am a strong advocate of being nice to yourself – but in a healthy way. You're going to hear me say this a lot. Find things that you can do for yourself that are treats, rewards and celebrations that are healthy. Sounds really simple doesn't it, but if you have been raised this way with cake or chips as a treat, trust me it's not.

We so often want to take the easy route, the quick route. In a society where we can access instant gratification in so many ways. If we are tired, hungry, work hard, hungover, stressed and we need a treat. What do we do? We reach for the easy option, junk food. Rather than booking that massage, relaxing, or getting ourselves to the yoga class, booking the theatre ticket, the dance class, coffee with a friend that makes you laugh. Because all of that takes a little bit more effort, but oh so much more rewarding and better for us as well. I challenge you to make more of an effort in your celebration and reward.

This is the same idea with alcohol as well, if you use alcohol as a reward, same principle.

Task

What do you currently treat yourself with?

Write a list and scale them 1-10 on how good for you they are. 10 being really healthy.

Example

Chips from the chip shop: 3

Sweets: 2

Takeaway: 2

MacDonald's: 1

Glass of wine: 2

Now if you have a list where you have things that you treat yourself with and very little is good for you, it's time to make some changes. Whether you want to lose weight or not. Remember this is about health, habit and how you feel. Do you feel good after eating rubbish?

Task

Write a list of all the things you can treat yourself with that are good for you

Scale them 1-10 on how likely you are to do them. 10 being the most likely.

Example

Have a massage: 3

Go to the gym or do some exercise: 5

Go for a swim: 5

Have a coffee with a friend: 6

Walk by the sea: 6

Watch a film: 7

Long hot bath: 2

I am sure you are aware and notice there is something about instant gratification there. If you buy it and it's in the house. It's easy to go to the cupboard, pull it out and eat/drink it. It's also easy to go to the shop and buy something. However it's not as quick and accessible to have a massage or go to the beach. It takes more effort as well. Let's be honest eating a huge packet of crisps is easy.

So watch out for this, if you are going for the instant gratification which most of us probably are. Stop...... and do something else.

Next time you want to treat yourself pick one of the activities you are most likely to do. There is no point having a list of things you can do to treat yourself if you are highly unlikely to do them. For instance, I love massages but realistically at the moment that's unlikely to happen, as I have to find somewhere to go and book it in, which will take time. However, I am likely to watch a film or visit a friend and have coffee.

You can feel healthier and gain control of your sugar or junk food habit. Lots of people do it every day, why should you be any different. You will feel a lot healthier and just generally better about yourself.

Thinking and torturing yourself with wanting to eat things that quite frankly have no nutritional value!! Eating them and then feeling terrible physically, mentally or both if you are really lucky.

Find the thing that works for you. What is it about eating healthily that motivates you? For some people its thinking of food as fuel, we put things into our body to help us live, grow, be healthy, think, excel, perform etc. Think of it as like putting coca cola in your car. Let's face it, you wouldn't. Your car definitely wouldn't run off this. So why do we put it our bodies?

There is a lovely quote I have seen recently that says, "we give our plants water to help them grow, so why do we give our children sugary drinks?" Good question.

I have a female friend who never struggles with her weight, she is very healthy and looks great. She doesn't especially enjoy food (now I am not suggesting that anyone feel like this about food, but it's interesting how it works for some people) she sees food as fuels, so she eats when she is hungry, when she needs to, to help her get through her busy day. And she eats a balanced diet because she knows that's what she needs.

When we focus on food as fuel we make very different choices. When we are hungry, we look at our choices of things to eat and ask ourselves what is the best thing for our mind and body to eat right now?

The choice is quite different to the one we would make if we weren't paying attention or going for the instant gratification.

You know the fuel that your car needs to keep it running well on the road. Giving your car, the right fuel helps it run well, need less repairs, cost you less and lasts longer. You do whatever you can to look after it. Why are you not making this same choice with your body and brain, your own chassis and engine? Now apply this to your body and brain. I think we all know by now we need a good mix of basic foods, whole foods, such as fruit, veg, meat, fish, grains and fats, with water. This is the fuel your body and brain need to help us grow, be strong, feel healthy, look good, help us work, learn and have fun.

Food is the Drug That I'm Thinking of

Although sugary/junk foods aren't drugs, they have turned into things we use in this way. Availability is a big one for a lot of people. Like alcohol, it is everywhere. In fact, it's probably more in visual sight than alcohol. What happens when you eat something like this is it triggers dopamine in the brain. This feels good for a short while, you want to repeat the feeling so some people just keep eating not paying attention to feeling full. We have some funny sayings in our house, "food is not love" is one of them. Make sure you are not filling a hole; do you feel empty and you just keep eating? What's missing?

Also like drugs sometimes people use food because they are unhappy. If this is you please be aware of this, are you eating on your emotions? Maybe because you are generally unhappy? What do you need to change in your life which will help you to support your health?

However sometimes eating bad food is just a habit.

I have some friends that when they got together in a relationship they stayed in and fed each other and put loads of weight on. There was no reason for it other than they liked eating. They were happy and in love. Nothing bad had happened, sometimes it's just because it's there and it tastes nice.

Remember what we said at the beginning of this chapter. The world has changed and we need to catch up. **Eat better quality foods and exercise more.** Educate yourself about food and learn about nutrient dense foods.

Picture This

Let's face it our brains are clever little things especially if we aren't paying attention. Most of us are visual, predominantly. So, with food being everywhere, on the TV, the internet, billboards; even if you are really doing well and making healthy choices at some point you are going to slip up, right?

Visually some of this stuff looks great, I bet you are doing it now, thinking about food? When we see it, a lot of us make pictures in our mind and that triggers our other senses.

How we feel, how it smells. We start salivating and before we know it we are on a full-blown craving. It is hard to resist.

If you are someone that likes to make pictures in your head, then stop yourself from doing it or play with the picture so it isn't so motivating. Like chocolate for instance, looks like poo. You won't forget that now. A friend of mine never ate chocolate because visually he said in his head it was poo, so he never ate it, clever.

For some people making the picture (in your head, visualization) really big works. I mean REALLY big, or very small so small it disappears like a pea. Changing it from colour to black and white, the list is endless. Mess around with your picture until something changes for the better.

If you have a particular thing you really struggle with, for example chocolate, cake or crisps etc, try a good master practitioner of NLP or hypnotherapist. You will only need 1 session, unless its connected to something deeper. Purely for kick-starting you to stop a particular thing it can really help. It gives you a boost, making it easier for you to take a break, stop, which in turn changes your taste buds and habits making everything a lot easier.

What Can You Do About it?

- Keep a record of your eating habits.
- Notice your patterns – change them – do something different: For instance, if you have cravings at 2pm then go for a walk at that time.
- Plan your eating: Planning works well with any behaviour change, at least in the first 3 months. Plan what you are going to cook and eat for the week.
- Replace rubbish food for healthier versions: There are so many healthy alternative recipes now on the internet. Some of them are quite good.
- Figure out what works and helps you stay motivated.
- Shop somewhere different: Go to the grocers for veg, the butchers for meat etc. Buy your food online.
- Use scaling prior to eating: On a scale of 1 – 10. Ask yourself whether you are hungry, indifferent or full. 1 is ridiculously hungry to the point of passing out, 5 is indifferent and 10 is so full you are going to be very ill. When I wake up in the morning I am probably a 4 and as time goes on I get to a 3. The idea is, that it gets you to eat before you get too hungry and stop before you have too much.
- Take your time: It takes time for our stomach to talk to our brains to register that we are full, it can take up to 20 mins. So, waiting can be good as well. If you are someone that binge eats this can be a good practice for you. 20m minutes is nothing.

- Build a routine so you are eating regularly but not in a binge pattern. You are eating a normal sized healthy meal and then you stop. And you wait for at least 2 hrs before you have anything else. Break the binge pattern.
- Take your time when you eat. Sit down, relax, make time for eating. Enjoy every mouthful.
- Chew your food properly. A really good nutritionist told me we should be chewing our food 30x.
- Use smaller plates: This is a really good one, it plays tricks with you and this is what we want to do. We are messing things up, messing with your habits, your patterns and how you see things. I don't know if you have noticed but some restaurants and people in their homes have huge plates and they fill them up because that's what everyone does, right? And then we are programmed to eat whatever is on our plate. So many reasons to eat up: it's a waste if you don't, so many other people need food etc. etc. the list goes on. All that social conditioning again. I once coached someone on a number of different things, mostly work performance. However he was unhappy with his weight and this came up sometimes but it wasn't the main issue for him. He wasn't massively over weight and did quite a lot of sport so neither of us was concerned about this. Throughout the coaching relationship as I coached him intensively for some time I got to know him well and was having lunch with him one day at his home, he cooked. I was amazed at the size of the plate and the

96

amount of food on it. So amazed that I probably didn't respond in the best way I could. (See no-one's perfect). I pointed out that the plate was huge and there were at least 2 meals on there for a grown man. I was truly horrified at the amount of food he was about to consume in one go. Then obviously was not surprised that he struggled with his weight. He then spent the next 10 minutes justifying the amount of food. He firmly believed that amount was ok. I left it, as that wasn't what we were working on. It's fascinating when you coach people and get to know them well, they tell you certain things and then you see the evidence of why they are the way they are. So, change your plates, to smaller ones, or just even normal sized ones for starters.

- Stick to a budget: Save the money you would normally spend on rubbishy junk foods and then treat yourself to something – new clothing, music, a night out, put it towards a holiday, a massage, an exercise class, an evening class or even better a healthy cooking class!!

- Reward: This one can be really motivating for people. If you are a big takeaway eater this is expensive. Every time you want one or would normally buy one, put the money in a jar, then at the end of the month or less count and empty the jar. Don't make yourself wait too long, it's not a punishment. It's supposed to be an incentive. Use it to do something from the alternative rewards we looked at earlier.

- Decide whether you need to moderate, control or stop eating rubbish altogether. Now only you know the answer to this one and sometimes its trial and error, each of us has different personalities. For instance, if I told myself I could never eat chocolate again I would go out and buy the biggest chocolate bar and eat all of it and feel very ill and disappointed in myself. However, if I tell myself I'm going to eat it occasionally then I do a lot better. I have to play a trick on myself. Are you someone that when they start eating these types of foods you don't have an off button. If this is you then it's best to go cold turkey for as long as you can, then plan a healthy/semi treat for around once a week if that feels good. It can be useful to cut out junk food for at least 7 days just to see how your taste buds change. Sugar is fascinating with this one. If you are a real sugar junkie, just cutting sugar out for this short amount of time can have a profound effect. I sometimes do a 7 day no sugar challenge in my Facebook group. Everyone says the same thing, when they do finally eat something sweet they say it tastes horrible. I know this myself as chocolate is one of my little distractions I need to keep an eye on. When I go 7 days without chocolate and then I eat some lovely dark super dooper choccy, it is so strong. It's too much and I can only eat a very small amount, as opposed to the whole shop when I am in full swing.

- Restrict yourself: Don't buy any rubbish. If you don't have it in the house you can't eat it. I have had people tell me they have to have it in the house for the kid's lunchbox! Now what is wrong with this sentence?? Why are you buying this stuff to feed your children, now I am not saying don't let them have it. But this is exactly it, maybe think of it as something to have on occasion. I think its Norway where this is reflected in the price of their foods. Healthy foods are cheaper than the rubbishy, junky sugary foods. Also I have heard people say they keep bad food in the house for their partner/husband/wife. Well I am sorry, people can support you in this for as long as needed. If they want to buy and eat rubbishy foods they can anytime, just not around you. If you only have healthy foods in the house it benefits the whole family.
- Using healthy alternatives can work well: There are so many recipes out there, some not so great I know. But some are good and full of wholefoods you can eat that's mostly healthy: homemade pizza, curry, cakes etc.
- Don't be too strict on yourself at the start: If you are going from a really bad eating pattern with a lot of rubbish start by eating healthy food regularly but don't worry too much about portion size. Allow yourself to eat as much as you want but make sure it's healthy. Then start regulating maybe a week later, otherwise big portions will continue to be normal for you – again you know best with this one. I once worked with someone

who had stopped using a lot of stimulants and started eating a lot. She needed to eat as she hadn't properly for a long time and part of getting better is sleeping and eating healthy food. Initially I advised to eat healthy food whenever she wanted. She did but it became too much and quickly turned into excessive and obsessive eating. She very quickly put a routine in to help her. She got very structured about times and meal planning to help with this difficult period.

- Drink water: If you need to, put a slice of lemon in it.
- Think ahead: This is a really good one. When we eat that thing that looks so yummy that isn't good for us we are thinking totally in the now, right in that moment. Which is great, but not when it comes to bad habits. When it comes to food think of the future: "If I eat this I am going to feel like this, it will affect my health in this way, etc. Back to the car metaphor. If I put this bad fuel in my car what will happen? It will break down!!" "What's the nutritional value of what I'm about to eat? What's my goal in terms of my eating? How does this help my goal?"
- Use a photo of how you want to look. Or maybe you need to use a photo of how you don't want to look. This will depend on what motivates you. Some of us are motivated away from. For instance if your motivation is to not be overweight, a picture of you looking larger than you would like will help to motivate you. However if you are motivated towards, it will be a picture of

someone or yourself looking how you want to look. Or buying a dress you want to wear but can't quite get into. Deep down inside you know which way motivates you more. I have a friend that buys dresses one size smaller to encourage herself to lose weight. She never does, she is not motivated towards. She is motivated away from.

Summary

Keep a diary or use an app, to keep track of your eating habits.

Change your outlook – "Food as fuel".

Mess with your habits and patterns – this one's really important.

Plan your eating.

Don't be too hard on yourself.

If in doubt drink water.

Use a photo.

Plan for the future: Every time you are about to eat something ask yourself if what you are doing now helps you achieve your current goals.

Use scaling, eat when you are hungry.

Get structured and consistent, if you have got out of the habit, put some routine in. Breakfast, lunch, dinner with snacks at similar times.

Ask yourself
If what you are doing now
helps you
achieve your current

goals.

8. Busyness, Stress and Tiredness

This section will explore busyness, stress and tiredness separately but they are all interlinked.

Busyness

We need to talk about busyness. If this is you: If you are always busy, always tired, don't get enough time for yourself, feel like you are doing everything for other people then you really need to address this. Busyness is a bad habit in itself. It seems to be a curse of modern day life, but you really need to remember that no one is doing this to you, you are doing it to yourself. This life is 100% your responsibility, no one is coming to save you. So, if you are too busy, too tired or all the above you are the only one that can change this.

Now I can hear you all shouting you have no idea what my life is like and no I don't, but I do know what life is like when things don't go as planned. Trust me, I really do. When things happen in your life that are out of our control, even then you can still find time for yourself. In fact it's even more important. I am going to say it again, this is your life! No one else's, you only get one chance, **this is it. It's happening now.**

There has been much written about what people regret about their life. What's interesting about that is people don't wish they had worked harder, finished their to do list or cleaned the house more.

Bronnie Ware has written a blog about her research into this.

The regrets touch upon being more genuine, not working so hard, expressing one's true feelings, staying in touch with friends and finding more joy in life."

- Bronnie Ware, The Top 5 Regrets of the Dying (Hay House)*
*For more information about Bronnie Ware and The Top 5 Regrets of the Dying visit hayhouse.com.au
http://hayhouse.com.au or http://bronnieware.com

When it really comes down to it, we know what is important. If you take 5 minutes out of your day, you know. Its things like, being with the people you love, doing the things you want, living life on your terms, experiencing things.

Your children don't care if you work hard, they care that you are happy and they get to spend time with you. Same as your friends and your family. I know I am making this sound easy, I know it's a balancing act, trust me I do. But what I want you to do is be aware of this. It's your life so it needs to work for you.

I know it needs to work for the people around you as well. But you can have bits in there that are for you. **What's your greatest regret so far, and what will you set out to achieve or change before you die?**

I want you to be really aware of this, **remember** no one ever regrets not working enough.

Task

Find somewhere quiet and take time to think. Imagine that you are 90 and you are looking back at your life. Write down what your life has been like. What sort or person have you been? What will people say about you? What have you achieved? What are you proud of? What does your life look like? Family? Friends? Significant other? Career? Where and how do you live? Fun and leisure? And so on, whatever is important to you. Just write and see what comes out.

Now look at this. How do you need to be living so that you have this life? Is what you are doing now, matching up with what you have written?

Busyness is a bad habit and addiction in itself. Think about it, you didn't intentionally choose for your life to be this busy to be this tired. Maybe there was a specific thing you wanted to do, so you squeezed it into your life. Maybe it's about your family, partner, work, and you will say things are out of your control.

I call bullshit!!! This may sound harsh, but it's true, you have allowed this to happen, no-one is forcing you. One of the things you can control in your life is choice. This is so powerful, I really need you to hear this. Choice: you choose what time you get up, you choose what you eat, where you work, what you do with your time. There may be some things in your life you can't control, but there will definitely be many things you can. So if you are super busy, very tired and would like things to change, you can make small changes, if you want. It is also well proven that you are not effective when you are too busy, there is a fine line between being efficient and fast and being too busy and tired.

Chopping Wood

Two men were chopping wood.

The younger man laboured hard and steadily all day long. The older man also worked hard but every so often would stop and take a break. While on his breaks he would call out to the younger man and say "come and have a rest, I want to show you something that will help you."

But the younger man would say "Not now I'm busy. I don't want to lose any time."

By the end of the day the elder man had chopped far more wood than the younger man. This was a great surprise to the younger man because he was sure he had worked harder than the elder man. So he asked "How did you do it? I mean how did you cut more wood than me?" And the elder man replied "Well, every time I stopped to take a break, I sharpened my axe!"

We should all take time to 'sharpen our axe'!

Over to You

It's your life, your choice. If you are too busy what are you going to do about it?

I want you to start by having a good honest look at your life. Get a piece of paper out and write down all the important areas of your life. Examples include:

- Work/career
- Family
- Partner
- Children
- Friends
- Health
- Leisure
- Fun
- Learning
- Religion
- Spirituality
- Personal development
- Money
- Sport/fitness

I could go on. But only you know the most important areas of your life.

Be honest with yourself, look at each area and scale them 1-10. 1 being not very good and 10 being amazing. Then ask yourself for each one how you could improve it. I also want you to pay attention to where you spend most of your time. Do you spend most of your time working or doing things for others? What is missing? What's the one thing you could change that would make a difference to you today? If you are tired because you are working too much, what can you do to work less and spend more time with your children or friends? If you can't change it now what can you do to change it in the near future? Giving it a time frame is really important.

If your problem is too much work and your boss won't support you, maybe you need to start looking for another job. Trust me no job is worth taking over your life, unless you are ok with it and its not causing you any problems, but the fact that you are reading this book tells that something is a problem.

When you have your list of areas and your answers to the questions above it will be really clear which 1 or 2 things will make the biggest difference to you today. Make plans to make one of those changes within the next week, or at least start the ball rolling.

There are other small changes you can make that will help:

- If you are tired, book time off just to rest. This is really important. A holiday that doesn't give you the time to relax defeats the object.
- Make sure you take at least 1 day off in the week to relax, if you can take 2 together even better. Sleep a little bit more, can you sneak in an extra hour a day on some days?
- Do some exercise. Nothing too strenuous, a hobby maybe, at least once a week. What this does is that it forces you to do something different and take time out.
- Start eating healthier and looking after yourself.

Just pick one of these things and start doing it, the more you do it the easier it will become.

Remember everything starts with a small change, but YOU make that small change happen, you have a choice.

#Keep it Simple.

sleep   eat   water

Stress

Busyness and stress can go hand in hand. Sometimes people are busy and stressed and then sometimes people are just stressed to the point where they have become ineffective. Stress can work in a number of ways. There are some people who are actually addicted to stress. It's how they work, they love it and it's their drug. If this is you please ask yourself if this is ok, that it isn't causing you any problems? If it isn't now it will be at some point. And it's highly likely that you are needing to use something to relax or come down off the stress: a glass of wine, beer, cigarette or drugs?

I once worked with a brilliant office manager, the best. However, she functioned on stress, she got off on the adrenaline rush. She was brilliant at her job, but at times her stress made her behave in ways that really effected the people around her. Because she was operating in a zone that was fast and efficient. She knew all the answers and her expectation was for others to be there as well. She was short and abrupt. Of course we are all different so not many people were on her wavelength. Daily she would upset someone, just by being abrupt and not thinking, prioritising her busyness.

Anyone who has worked in a team, particularly a fast, effective team, knows you need to get on. Harmony is important, we don't have to love each other, respect is a good start though. She would have said she wasn't stressed, just busy and she knew she was good at her job. However if she had known how other people felt about her she would have been mortified.

She had no awareness of the impact her stress/busyness was having on the people around her, because she was so fixed, blinkered on her zone. The price was not only her working relationships, it was also her emotional health, and quite often she would crash. There would be an event, she would be unable to see that her way of being was part of the issue and would feel hurt, devastated at times that people didn't like her. I firmly believe that she could have been just as effective in fact more so if she wasn't so in her stress zone.

If she wasn't stressed her communication would have been completely different. People would have responded to her very differently, improving everyone's working environment which in turn would help her improve her efficiency and work. And also significantly improving those relationships. Ultimately that's what she wanted, to get on with people. See we don't work in isolation even if we think we do, or we think that everyone else is incompetent. Actually we are just all different and bring different things to the table.

What is Stress?

The Oxford English dictionary definition is:

"a state of mental or emotional strain or tension resulting from adverse or demanding circumstances"

When you have a "stress response" to a situation your body makes more adrenaline (also called epinephrine) and cortisol, the primary stress or survival hormones. When the stress or threat is gone, the hormones and their actions go back to normal levels. Adrenaline is the hormone that makes your heart race, causes you to breathe fast and makes you feel anxious when you encounter stress. This hormone increases as part of a programmed response activated to help you manage what your body perceives as an immediate threat. If your stress is ongoing however, this response is prolonged and may convert an initial protective mechanism into negative effects on your health.

Adrenaline Production
The adrenaline response to stress is transmitted through the automatic nervous system to nerve endings and the adrenal glands. To increase adrenaline production and secretion, stress activates a complex reaction, that involves:

- Activation of the locus coreolos, the hypothalamus and other areas in the brain that control and coordinate the adrenaline stress response.

Activation of the sympathetic nervous system, part of the complex autonomic nervous system which includes nerve cells, nerve pathways and nerve endings in the spinal cord, brain, your adrenal glands and other organs.

- Signals to the region of adrenal glands called the medulla, which lies in the middle area of the glands, carried through the autonomic nervous system cells and pathways.

- The hormone (neurotransmitter) noradrenaline (norepinephrine) which transmits signals to the brain, the sympathetic nervous system and the adrenal glands and from which adrenaline is made.

- Other hormones such as cortisol

When stress activates this complex system it increases the enzyme that converts noradrenaline to adrenaline in the adrenal medulla and the blood level of adrenaline as well as noradrenaline (catecholamines) rise.

How you respond to stress and how much adrenaline and other hormones increase depends partly on: how you cope with stress, your life experiences and your genetics.

Cortisol

At the same time as the above, stress activates the hypothalamic -pituitary-adrenal axis (HPA) to increase production of cortisol from the outer region of the adrenal gland called the cortex. Cortisol is also essential to the increase in the enzyme that converts noradrenaline to adrenaline.

The Role of Adrenaline in Stress

Adrenaline is part of the so-called "fight-flight response to stress that protects you from harm. Adrenaline normally helps to maintain your body's basic functions (homeostasis) and affects every organ in the body. Increased production and release of adrenaline in response to acute stress enhances its protective functions but may also be detrimental to t hose at risk.

In response to acute stress, increased adrenaline mostly speeds things up and leads to:

- Heightened awareness and alertness to deal with the stressful situation.

- Increased energy to fight or run.

- Increased heart rate and force of contraction of the heart, which in a person with heart disease could trigger a heart attack.

- Increase blood pressure which could also trigger a stroke or heart attack in a susceptible person.

- Increased breathing to provide more oxygen to your tissues.

- Mobilizes glycogen (starch) from your liver to convert it to glucose for energy.

- Increased perspiration.

- Decreased response to pain.

- Decrease in bowel function.

Cortisol plays its own role in protecting you, including providing fuel for your muscles and brain. These responses all arm you to survive episodes of stress or any other threat to your body.

Adaptation Response

Adrenaline and cortisol and other parts of the stress response also play a beneficial role in helping a person adapt and manage stressful episodes. However, when the response is not turned off, or when it is repeatedly triggered, then the adaptive (coping) mechanism is overloaded and may not be effective.

Effect of Sustained Stress

Under sustained stress, your adrenaline and other stress hormones stay elevated and you might feel that you are constantly under siege. The initially protective adrenal response to stress can become detrimental to your health and your feeling of well-being by its continued presence.

Too much and prolonged adrenaline and stress can lead to physical, behavioural and psychological disorders including:

- Heart disease such as an enlarged heart, heart failure and irregular heartbeat.

- High blood pressure.

- Stroke from high blood pressure.

- Irritable bowel.

- Eating disorders from disturbed bowel function.

- Weakened immune system.

- Autoimmune diseases.

- Headaches.

- Anxiety, irritability, shakiness.

- Depression.

- Sleep disturbance.

- Lack of motivation and drive secondary to anxiety and depression.

- Skin disorders such as psoriasis and other skin rashes.

- Memory and learning impairment.

- Accelerated aging.

Stress information taken from
http://stress.lovetoknow.com/about-stress/stress-adrenaline

Vilma Ruddock MD

Now we are all different and we all respond differently to different situations and throughout our day we will experience situations that can make us feel stress. Crossing the road, simple things. Not all stress is bad. It's important to establish whether it is your busy schedule that is causing your stress or other factors. Be honest with yourself and take a look at what you can change to make things feel better.

For any type of stress **ask yourself these questions:**

- Are you addicted to stress?
- Do you enjoy it?
- Is it your reason/excuse to: drink, eat rubbish, smoke or party hard?
- Is your stress making you feel ill?
- Is it making you feel tired every day?

- Is stress a negative emotion for you? If so do you spend a lot of time feeling negative?
- What is the source of your stress? Or have you just got into a bad habit?
- If there is a valid reason for your stress, what can you do to improve this, change it?

What Can I Do About It?

The after-effects of acute stress or multiple, daily, chronic or repeated stresses (including accompanying sleep deprivation), can rob you of your sense of well-being and make you sick. Strategies for reducing your stress can include:

- Change or control what you can. E.g. It might be your job. You love your work, you love what you do, but it's just too much. It's become stressful and you have gotten into a habit of being stressed when you are there and doing whatever you need to come down from the stress. You have tried getting support from your manager but they are either not listening or they have too much of their own to deal with. Either way that's not an option, you have tried to make it work but you have reached a point where you know you need to get another job. There are things at work that just aren't working for you and you don't have the power to change them. You might have loved it originally. You might like the people there. You might care about it, feel loyal. But at what price? Accept what you can't change, if it's still not working, let it go and start looking for another job.

- Get enough sleep, sleep is so important.
- Eat a healthy diet: It's easy to use bad food when you are stressed and busy, too easy. But this will only make you feel worse. If you are someone that gets unwell a lot because of the stress you are under, this is even more important. Take time for making healthy meals and buying healthy snacks.
- Exercise: This is really important, it focuses your mind on other things and releases endorphins. It doesn't have to be strenuous: a walk, swim, dance, exercise class or yoga is good. Pick one and make yourself go at least once a week. Notice how that helps and then go more. Ideally you want to be doing it 3 x a week.
- Learn and practice relaxation techniques which can trigger the "relaxation response" and diminish the responses to stress such as rapid heart rate, high blood pressure and anxiety.
- Build a support network of people you can trust and rely on.
- Engage in activities or learn a new skill that brings you joy.

In addition, don't hesitate to seek help from a coach who can help you better understand your sources of stress and how to better cope with them and improve your well-being.

It is possible to feel different. But you do need to take charge and do something to help yourself.

But What If Its Beyond My Control?

Sometimes life is difficult and there is genuinely nothing you can do it about it. If this is the case, then you really need to put things in place so other areas of your life are ok. Make it easier on yourself.

For example, you might be going through a particularly messy divorce or have an ex-partner who is intent on making contact with the children difficult. This can go on for some time, even years in some cases. You can't control the other partner or change them. However, it is really important in this situation that you stay measured and balanced for the children, whether you feel like it or not. Because not only are you in an incredibly difficult situation emotionally and probably financially, you need to maintain some level of a good life for the children and reduce the impact of a difficult situation on them. In this case it's important that other areas of your life are ok, such as work. Make sure this is ok and manageable, if not maybe it's time to get another job, one you enjoy with people that will support you.

Or maybe you are caring for someone; this can be really hard. Maybe you have a partner with a long term illness or a child with behavioural problems. You have committed and accepted your situation, you are there because you love the person and you want to look after them. However it's tough. Life can be hard. Everyday could be difficult and you don't see an end. This is where it becomes incredibly important to find time for moments of pleasure throughout the day so you don't stay in that stressed state. Take some time off from it.

Moments where you can forget your difficult situation are so important. Spend time with friends and family, relaxing and socialising. Do nice things and take time off. Your life may be difficult and there is nothing you can do about that. But you can make sure that you have a nice time as often as you can. Please do not underestimate the importance of this. Don't stay in the difficult situation 24 hours a day. Doing something you love can be a godsend here. Something that truly takes you away from the problem, even if it's for 1 hr. Dancing, listening to music, running, swimming, painting, playing games, watching a film, reading a book, any activity you love that helps you to escape the difficult situation and feel good when you do it. It's like taking a little mini holiday. A holiday from things that are difficult that you can't change. Like we said if you are in it 24hrs a day and this goes on and on and you can't take a proper holiday or change it. Then you need to be taking mini holidays during the day.

In these situations, learn to manage the stress. It will pass, have faith, even something that seems impossible can sort its self out.

Jennifer's Story of Change

Jennifer was slap bang in the middle of a difficult divorce. Her ex-husband was very angry at the separation and divorce and wasn't thinking straight. He had got himself into that blind rage. He was willing to do anything to make life difficult for her. When I met her she was in a bad place, on her knees with what she was dealing with and trying her hardest to not succumb to taking something to manage it. She was feeling every last bit of the fear, anxiety and stress of the situation she was in. Because of what was happening between her and her ex-husband her children were suffering in different ways, they were really struggling. The eldest was dealing with panic and anxiety, the youngest was unable to manage his emotions and behaviour. His behaviour was so bad she spent a lot of time talking with school; they couldn't keep him in a class. When he was at home he would smash things up, shout, scream, swear, be violent and she would spend a lot of time restraining him for his own safety. He was only 6 years old at the time and she knew she needed help. She got some help from her local children's mental health team and it was through this work she came to accept and learn that she and her ex-husband had created this. Her son was communicating his situation through his behaviour. She also learned and accepted that her fear, anxiety and stress was making his behaviour worse and if there was going to be any chance to help him change it, she needed to start with herself.

She was in a bad place, really struggling, working hard trying to keep everything together. Crying a lot, contemplating suicide as she couldn't see another way out. Her biggest fear was that this is what her life had become, caring for her child with emotional behavioural problems. In this situation there were 4 people and she could only change herself. She could support her children, but she couldn't change her ex-husband and what was happening, she had no power over this. The first step was accepting this situation then working on the bits she could change and work with. Finding the choice within a difficult situation is really important.

With support, she worked on herself, hard, so she wasn't in a permanent state of fear, anxiety and stress. She then got help for her eldest so he could help himself. Then she started the journey of learning how to work with her youngest's behaviour.

It was a difficult journey, but after a few years' things started to improve. Take note here it took years for things to improve, now I am not saying all change takes years, it doesn't, but being aware of patience and persistence will help.

The important bit was she started with herself as this was the bit she could control, working on her own emotions. The other bit that was crucial here was that she looked at her whole life and changed the other bits that were hard. She had a very difficult job at the time, so she changed it to a much easier one. It was still a good job with people she liked, but very easy on her emotionally. She did quite a lot of exercise to help manage the negative emotions. This really helps. That thing about finding bits in your day where you can feel different, exercise really does that. She made sure she spent time with her friends. She found a hobby that she loved and this was the icing on the cake, no matter how hard things got, she could escape to the things she loved to do.

I can't stress enough, the importance of taking time out of your difficult life to experience pleasure and joy. If your life is difficult because of a situation you can't change, find the bits you can change, find moments, 5 mins, 20 mins, 1 hr, the occasional day where you can do something that brings you joy. These moments are your holiday, your time off. At the time is doesn't feel like it but when it's over its easy to see what you have learnt from a situation.

I know its corny bit it really is true. What doesn't kill you makes you stronger. I can very clearly see the benefits of what I have learnt when I have had to deal with difficult situations in my life, even for long periods of time. I have also seen this with other people, the people who have had to overcome something are a lot more patient, tolerant, measured, take life in their stride. Don't sweat the small stuff basically and as a result they are happier and more content, regardless of their life situation.

What If It Is in My Control?

Hopefully by now you will have identified if the source of your stress is something you can control or not.

If you can change the reason for your stress, it causes you problems and you don't want to change it, ask yourself why not?

I mean really, why are you allowing yourself to have a difficult time?

Are you punishing yourself for something?

What is stopping you from making the changes?

These are valid questions I want you to ask yourself. It really is that simple.

Usually when I work with people and this one comes up and it does quite a bit, they can clearly tell me why they are punishing themselves. Why they are not allowing their life to move forward. It could be something that happened some time ago that they feel responsible for. Sometimes it is just a feeling from an event, and they don't even know if the other people involved feel the same way. It could be something that was big for you, is now irrelevant or even unremembered for the other people. You have no way of knowing unless you ask. You are not a mind reader, unless someone tells you how they feel you don't know what an event or a situation means to them. The big piece of advice for past events is very simple: you can't change the past, (I mean really you can't, please take this on board) **YOU CAN'T CHANGE THE PAST**. But you can affect the here and now and your future.

It's up to you and YOU need to take the steps to make it happen. If you ask anyone that has any success in their life or something that is going well, it's because they put the effort in, it didn't happen by accident, (well sometimes it does, but mostly people work at it).

People who are fit and healthy, eat healthy food and exercise. People who have happy well rounded-children, they are good parents, they put the time in.

People who are successful in their career, they have put the time in worked at it.

Anyway you get the point.

So work out what you need to do and do it.

Summary

Start with small changes. Give yourself a timeframe to hold you accountable.

Can you change it?

What can you do to look after yourself so it doesn't affect you negatively?

If you can, change it?

What can you do?

Small changes?

Timeframe it?

 If you don't want to why not?

Are you punishing yourself?

Why are you punishing yourself?

Are you enjoying it?

Are you just addicted to the stress? Nice little stress, bad habit addiction?

Using another bad habit on top to manage your stress, pain killers, alcohol, smoking, junk food, party drugs becoming a bad habit.

Things you can control:

1. Your beliefs
2. Your attitude
3. Your thoughts
4. Your perspective
5. How honest you are
6. Who your friends are
7. What books you read
8. How often you exercise
9. The type of food you eat
10. How many risks you take
11. How you interpret situations
12. How kind you are to others
13. How kind you are to yourself
14. How often you say "I love you"
15. How often you say "thank you"
16. How you express your feelings
17. Whether or not you ask for help
18. How often you practice gratitude
19. How many times you smile today
20. The amount of effort you put forth
21. How you spend/invest your money
22. How much time you spend worrying
23. How often you think about your past
24. Whether or not you judge other people
25. Whether or not you try again after a setback
26. How much you appreciate the things you have

BY RUBEN CHAVEZ // THINKGROWPROSPER

Tiredness

Do not underestimate this one. It's a funny little one; well not so funny. For some reason in modern society we just don't give it the credit it deserves. I know I haven't over the years and I've watched many other people do the same.

"I'm tired, too busy" it's their mantra.

Is that really ok? What are you going to do about it?

It's simple: take time out, stop and sleep for a bit.

I cannot underestimate the importance of sleep. Feeling tired really effects a lot of things in our lives. Particularly these days we don't seem to place much importance on sleep. Everything is so fast paced, we put ourselves under imaginary pressure, because we are our own hardest taskmasters.

Feeling tired effects our physical health our emotional health, how our day goes, how we respond to different events. If you have made changes, stopped drinking, smoking, using drugs. When you are tired its harder to say no to things.

I worked with a lady that did a very high powered job for a while. By accident she had sort of fell into it. A natural progression on the career ladder. I am sure a few of us have done this. Just getting on with life not really paying attention. She actively chose the original job, and then the roles changed, the contracts changed and a few years in she found herself doing something else altogether.

Long hours, lots of responsibility, great opportunity, but much of it just wasn't working for her. She found herself working very long hours and constantly feeling tired and always thinking about the job. She realised that something needed to change. She wasn't available for the children and being a single mum this was hard. With no partner to take over for a while so she could see whether it could work out for her.

The children started to complain. You're always on your laptop mum or always on the phone. Ultimately it came down to this for her, her children where more important than any job and honestly, she wasn't enjoying it. When she was honest with herself, she didn't enjoy 1 day in the job and this went on for some time.

In the past she had a drink and drug problem but when she came to me she had been healthy for a good number of years. This was the first time in many years that she had thought about drinking and using everyday. She knew herself well enough to know that all it was going to take was a perfect storm. A day when it was really bad, bumping into the wrong/right person whichever way you want to look at it and that would be it. And she really didn't want to drink or take drugs just because she was tired and struggling with the hours. She was honest with herself enough to know that she was at a point where the cravings and potential triggers were an accident waiting to happen.

Her response was let's drink or use to cope with it, so she knew something was wrong. She was tired and unhappy, it was the job. But society does this weird thing to our expectations. She was a single mum, so yes, it's great to have a good job that pays a lot. Security, having money to do things, provide for your children, is a great feeling. Also, it's a good job, she should feel lucky that she has this opportunity? Right?

When she came to me I asked her a few key questions.

"How are you?" I asked, "tired very tired", she answered.

"Why?" I asked, "It's the job, the hours are too long for me to sustain for any length of time", she answered.

"Do you enjoy your job?" I asked, "No", she answered.

"Why are you doing it?" I asked.

And there we had it, really simple, why are you spending 10/12 hours a day doing something you don't like?

Why?

Sounds silly doesn't it when you see it in black and white and it's about someone else.

But seriously if you can identify with this and you are spending a lot of time doing something you don't enjoy and you can change it, why?

When we started to unpack this, we uncovered all sorts of limiting beliefs she had picked up from elsewhere that she knew weren't real for her.

"I should feel grateful it's a good job"

"A real chance for someone like me". What does that even mean. Anything is possible for anyone and she really did believe this.

"Not every job is easy?" No not every job is easy, it can still be difficult and you can enjoy the challenge, however to not enjoy any part of it is different.

"This is the natural progression, this is what society expects of me."

I am sure when we all think about it carefully we also have some of these and different ones too. Be aware of them, they may not be yours and you may not believe them.

"You have to work hard for your money" is another one.

We looked at whether they were beliefs for her and when we really looked at them they weren't, they didn't serve her any purpose. It's just a job, why should she feel grateful, there are lots of other jobs, she is good at her job and that's why they gave it to her.

Society doesn't expect anything anymore, we have so moved on from this one. There are no rules. Even for women and particularly for western women (in terms of freedom and choice we really do have it good), each person can make up their own rules. Again, it's your life.

It doesn't make any difference if it is a good job with great money and prospects, if you don't like it and its making you miserable really what's the point.

She worked with me for about 6 weeks and it helped her come to understand that there was absolutely no need for her to be there, no reason, no benefit for her at all and she was able to leave and feel good about it. Taking time off to rest and relax.

The original issue was tiredness and a lot of people are tired. For so many reasons: work, family, children, caring, the list goes on. We seriously underestimate what being tired does to us emotionally and what we do to cope with it. Stimulants, coffee, tea, cigarettes, sugary food, junk foods, alcohol to relax with, the list is endless.

Sometimes we just get out of the habit of sleeping and rest. Particularly if we have had a difficult period with working too much. Looking after babies and small children etc.

Stop

On a scale of 1-10, 10 being very tired ask
yourself honestly how tired you are, today?

And generally, how tired are you? This year?

What Can I Do About It?

Believe it or not, most people can teach themselves to sleep. There are things you can do to help yourself.

I have lost count of the amount of people I have worked with, who tell me they are having trouble sleeping. But they really aren't doing anything to help themselves. It's as if by magic they expect to be able to just sleep. Drinking lots of coffee, not taking any exercise, poor diet, over stimulated, caught in the busyness trap, not making time to relax and the list goes on.

Once people focus and follow the advice below, consistently (that's the important bit, until they teach themselves) they have no trouble sleeping.

I would like to remind you of when you first learnt to drive, or first learnt anything for that matter. You learnt what to do, you kept doing the same thing, until it became easier and more natural, but it took time. Mirror, signal, manoeuvre, clutch, break, accelerator, so much to do in one go. It was hard, but you kept going.

Swimming, particularly front crawl, the breathing with the arms and legs, takes time, you have to keep practicing.

This is the same.

When people first stop using a relaxant, such as alcohol and cannabis. They have to take the time to re-programme themselves. Because they have got used to using something that in the short term is relaxing their body and helping them get to sleep. You have been accessing the short cut. Using something to help you relax quickly, rather than doing something to help you relax.

If you are having trouble sleeping there are a few simple things you can do to help yourself:

- **Get into a routine:** Sticking to a schedule allows your body to set its internal rhythm so you can get up at the time you want, consistently, every single day. Also, make sure you try to keep the same schedule on weekends too, otherwise the next morning, you will wake later and feel overly tired.
- **Sleep only at night.** Avoid daytime sleep if possible. Daytime naps steal hours from night time slumber. Limit daytime sleep to 20-minute power naps.
- **Exercise:** Activity works wonders for your sleep. Your body uses the sleep period to recover its muscles and joints that have been exercised. Twenty to thirty minutes of exercise every day can help you sleep, but be sure to exercise in the morning or afternoon. Exercise stimulates the body and aerobic activity before bedtime may make falling asleep more difficult. If you can exercise outside, even if it's just a good walk, fresh air helps too.
- **Taking a hot shower or bath:** Doing this before bed helps bring on sleep because they can relax tense muscles.
- **Avoid eating just before bed.** Give yourself at least 2

hours from when you eat to when you sleep. This allows for digestion to happen (or at least start) well before you go to sleep so your body can rest well during the night, rather than churning away your food.

- **Learn about foods that will aid sleep:** Carbs are good to have in the evening as they help to increase serotonin, which aids sleep at night. Tryptophan is an amino acid that helps aid sleep because it helps to make serotonin. Foods rich in Tryptophan include turkey, oats and almonds. Warm homemade almond milk before bed is a great sedative. Magnesium is possible the most important mineral for sleep and relaxation. Dark leafy veg are rich in magnesium as are nuts and seeds. A magnesium supplement for sleep can be really helpful. *Information from Gwen Warren Biting Fit.*

- **Avoid caffeine:** It keeps you awake and that's not what you want for a good night's sleep. Maybe only have 1 cup in the morning. Definitely not after midday.   This includes fizzy drinks and energy drinks, there is a lot of caffeine in these. Make sure you read the labels if you drink random fizzy drinks.

- **Avoid Alcohol:** Alcohol might help you nod off, but even just a couple of drinks can affect the quality of your sleep. People usually tell me they wake up the next day feeling like they haven't slept at all.

- **Read a fiction book:** It takes you to a whole new world if you really get into it. And then take some time to ponder over the book as you fall asleep.   It really helps you to relax and unwind. If you struggle with reading try audio books.

- **Sleep in silence:** Sleeping with no music or TV on is easier and more restful. Sleep with no distractions is best for a clearer mind

- **Hypnotherapy:** Download a good session onto your phone or iPod. I have met many people who tell me hypnotherapy doesn't work for them. I have sent them a simple 20-minute relaxation session and they tell me they fell asleep during the session. Use it as part of your routine, at the end of the day.

Now I know this all sounds simple, but I have worked with a lot of people and a large number of them have told me they have problem sleeping. Mostly it's because they have got into bad habits. They are drinking too much, eating too much rubbish, not exercising, drinking too much weapons grade coffee. They have been using something to get to sleep with. Or they are stressed and their brain is working overtime and they are finding it hard to relax.

If it's all a bit daunting for you, start small. Pick the one thing on the list that you think will make the biggest difference to how you are feeling and see how that goes.

If you have tried all the tips and you have really persevered with a routine and it still not helping with your sleep, I mean really

tried. I highly recommend finding yourself a good sleep therapist.
They will do all of the above and take it a bit further.

In my experience, though very few people need this. Give it at least 3 weeks of doing everything you need to give you the best chance.

The other thing maybe that there are some underlying reasons such as worries that won't go away or intrusive thoughts. If this is you have tried all of the above and you know that there is something in your head that is keeping you awake. Find yourself a good life coach or therapist that can work with you on your worries/thoughts. It is possible to learn how to work with your thoughts and feelings to help you.

9. Boredom

Another reason I hear a bit (not so much I have to say) but we need to cover it just in case. "Is I am bored" or "but it's boring when I don't drink" etc. So this one comes in a number of forms.

There is the busyness trap, so people are so busy and get into bad habits about this as we have previously talked about. But really if they start making changes what do they do? How do you relax? Do nothing?

I hear people tell me they don't know what to do with themselves. How to just be, (on which there are many books written).

Some people who use alcohol, drugs, food because they haven't got anything better to do and they are using it as an excuse, well if I come home from work I have nothing else to do so I drink or take drugs.

Here is another perspective from Gayatri Devi associate professor of English.

https://www.theguardian.com/commentisfree/2015/sep/28/boredom-cures-privilege-free-mind

We might feel like confessing to boredom is confessing to a character-flaw. Popular culture is littered with advice on how to shake it off: find like-minded people, take up a hobby, find a cause and work for it, take up an instrument, read a book, clean your house and certainly don't let your kids be bored: enrol them in swimming, soccer, dance, church groups – anything to keep them from assuaging their boredom by gravitating towards sex and drugs. To do otherwise is to admit that we're not engaging with the world around us. Or that your cell phone has died.

But boredom is not tragic. Properly understood, boredom helps us understand time, and ourselves. Unlike fun or work, boredom is not about anything; it is our encounter with pure time as form and content. With ads and screens and handheld devices ubiquitous, we don't get to have that experience that much anymore. We should teach the young people to feel comfortable with time.

I live and teach in small-town Pennsylvania, and some of my students from bigger cities tell me that they always go home on Fridays because they are bored here.

You know the best antidote to boredom, I asked them? They looked at me expectantly, smartphones dangling from their hands. Think, I told them. Thinking is the best antidote to boredom. I am not kidding, kids. Thinking is the best antidote to boredom. Tell yourself, I am bored. Think about that. Isn't that interesting? They looked at me incredulously. Thinking is not how they were brought up to handle boredom.

When you're bored, time moves slowly. The German word for "boredom" expresses this: langeweile, a compound made of "lange," which means "long," and "weile" meaning "a while". And slow-moving time can feel torturous for people who can't feel peaceful alone with their minds. Learning to do so is why learning to be bored is so crucial. It is a great privilege if you can do this without going to the psychiatrist.

So lean in to boredom, into that intense experience of time untouched by beauty, pleasure, comfort and all other temporal salubrious sensations. Observe it, how your mind responds to boredom, what you feel and think when you get bored. This form of metathinking can help you overcome your boredom, and learn about yourself and the world in the process. If meditating on nothing is too hard at the outset, at the very least you can imitate William Wordsworth and let that host of golden daffodils flash upon your inward eye: emotions recollected in tranquillity – that is, reflection – can fill empty hours while teaching you, slowly, how to sit and just be in the present.

Don't replace boredom with work or fun or habits. Don't pull out a screen at every idle moment. Boredom is the last privilege of a free mind. The currency with which you barter with folks who will sell you their "habit," "fun" or "work" is your clear right to practice judgment, discernment and taste.

In other words, always trust when boredom speaks to you. Instead of avoiding it, heed its messages, because they'll keep you true to yourself.

It might be beneficial to think through why something bores you. You will get a whole new angle on things. Hold on to your boredom; you won't notice how quickly time goes by once you start thinking about the things that bore you.

It's Time to Relax

Do you spend time relaxing?

I mean really relaxing? No stimulus at all? Doing something that relaxes you or even better nothing at all?

How often do you spend time relaxing?

Do you take regular time off?

In the week?

Every day?

In the year?

When I managed a team that worked incredibly hard in a very difficult area of work I would always encourage them wherever possible to take 2 weeks off together. If you are a super busy person 1 week isn't really enough.

When you book your much needed week off it takes a good few days to wind down, stop waking up at 4, 5, or 6. Whatever your pattern is. It might even take 5 days to get used to relaxing. Just being, not doing much.

Now I am making this sound easy and if you are Mr or Mrs Super busy this really isn't, I know. If you have listened and done the work in the other chapters then you are ready for this. You will know what you are doing and why and which bits you need to change. So this is just the icing on the cake.

In this crazy modern world some of us live on a conveyor belt never stopping to smell the roses, just relaxing can be excruciating. I know, I am the worst culprit. So, if I can do it anyone can, I challenge you!!

We have lost the art, the habit. And yes you guessed it that's all it really is. We have pushed more and more into our lives, got into bad habits and started using substances to help us manage our busy lives.

It's time to get a grip.

If we keep going like this, the problem seeps out somewhere. I promise you I see it all the time. People have lives like this and something happens. Either they get ill, something goes wrong in their relationships, children struggle, work doesn't go so well, financial problems, just generally feeling rubbish or even worse the big event happens that really causes us problems.

Just because we are tired, stressed, using substances, not paying attention or everything is going too fast.

By now you will have figured out what the biggest issue is for you and what you need to start changing. Maybe you have even started making changes. Great. The next thing to take on board is mastering relaxing……. "Just be".

Just Be

It's tough to "just be" anymore. Why can't we stop for moment and see things for the actual way that they are? Why do we have to keep ourselves busy, obsessed, and "passionate" all of the time?

For many people the thought of stopping to feel anything that is real in their lives is a distant afterthought to all of the projects and actions that they have forced upon themselves (or been forced upon by others). I know that this is the case for myself. I'd most times much rather check things off a list that I can make endless for myself than stopping, getting out of work mode, and see my surroundings for what they really are. If I stop to take a look at what things truly are, then I may have to make a change in my life and change is hard.

The thing that we forget to realize is that this "stopping and being" is just another part of being productive. If we don't face the fear of seeing things for the way that they truly are because of the perceived pain of change, then we could be setting ourselves up to take on projects, actions, and even goals that don't mean a damn to us.

Fear of the uncertain

Fear is a strong motivator, but it tends to be in the opposite way that we would like. Fear of uncertainty is another reason we have a difficult time stopping and being. I'm always freaked out that I won't have enough money to take care of me and my loved ones. This uncertainty of the future motivates me to do things that are possibly not the greatest for me, like take and keep jobs that promise me decent money but don't give me personal satisfaction in return, or take on side work that I know will help pay for things, but could leave me little time for anything else.

We don't completely know what tomorrow will bring. Or even a minute from now. But that is a constant. We can plan for that uncertainty and face it.

What to do about it

The tips below are practical and possibly obvious, but that's a good thing. The fact is that they work, but only if you work them. Most people won't work them – they will scan over them and continue on. If you are experiencing the fear mentioned above, don't scan these and move on. Try them out.

1. Plan times to stop and be for a moment every day, multiple times a day. You don't have to be Buddha, here. Simply stop for a moment outside of your email, phone, notifications, and anything else that keeps you busy. Stop and breathe deep through your stomach. You can think whatever you want to think, just try to come back to your deep breaths.

2. Plan times to write every day. You don't have to be a poet or auto biographer, here. Simply get out pen and paper or your trusty plain-text editor and write your ass off. You can write about anything that you like. You may find some of these fears mentioned above start to come out. It's a good think to notice them as it's the only way to face them.

3. Plan times to be with your friends and family every day. You don't have to be the Partridge family or everyone's BFF, here. Simply hang out with the people you love and remember why you love them. Also, remind yourself why they love you. We tend to think a lot about ourselves and not enough about others that are important.

4. Plan time to plan for a moment every day. You don't have to be a professional project manager. Simply take a look at your workload that is front of you (helps when you have that already defined!) and make decisions on what can stay, what can be gotten rid of, and what you should really be working on next. Focus. This step is much, much easier and closer to what you want and need to do when it is followed by the above three steps.

Stopping the rat race of your productive life can be tough. Especially since it feels that you never have enough time or energy to get everything done. The thing is that you may not need to get it all done. The only way to find this out is to face your fears of what is real and your uncertainty of the future by stopping and being everyday. Only then can you make the decision of what work you should keep in your life.

CM Smith – Lifehacks

http://www.lifehack.org/articles/lifestyle/fear-why-we-cant-just-be.html

Time Counts

Here's the thing with time, we can fill it up, we can be super busy, very tired and still not get it all done and does it really matter? If you had 3 months to live what matters?

Seriously ask yourself. **Ask yourself now if you had 3 months to live what would you do?**

- Write it down.

I know it's not cleaning the cooker, doing the garden, getting the promotions. I don't know about you. But for me it's dancing, having fun, giving back in some way, seeing the world, being with friends and family.

My daily list doesn't come into it.

So if you're daily list doesn't matter, if most of what you are doing you wouldn't do if you had 3 months to live? What do you want to do with your time? What is important to you?

It's your life after all……. It's your time.

Whats the 1 thing you can do today that will make the biggest difference to your life?

I love this question, I use it a lot for a lot of things. It really helps you focus on what is important.

Before you get into: cleaning cooking, washing, emails, work, doing things for others.

I am not saying don't do those things.

I am saying make your life work for you.

Maybe the 1 thing you can do today is eat healthy, sleep a bit more, do less.

Imagine what your day would be like if you did these simple things.

Balance.

10. Relationships

After reading this book you are going to want to change some aspects of your life. This is hard to do without the support of those around you.

There could be many reasons why this is a problem for you. I will try and tackle some of the issues in this section.

Family

Here, I am talking about extended family: parents, aunts, uncles, cousins etc. It may be that there is a culture of drinking, eating bad food within your extended family. It might even be that someone has a problem with being overweight or unhealthy. But because people are uneducated about these things for an older generation it really isn't seen as an issue. This is particularly true for the baby boomers. Baby boomers are the ones that are causing society the most issues in terms of a drain on health services. They may have always had a drink, growing up like that, but not had any serious issue so why should they stop? It might be just as they get older that they are noticing some health issues. If you are in this age range or have family that are, you and they may be having issues caused by long term innocuous drinking. Over acidity in the stomach, ulcers, skin problems, overweight, not sleeping properly, feeling sluggish, anxiety and depression, the list goes on. These are the kind of lower level health issues that someone might just pass off as an effect of ageing.

But stop right there If you reduce or stop your drinking, partying, for a while or change your diet you will feel better. I guarantee.

If you want to make changes it can be hard being around family if they are like this. And it's a similar case with friends or any people who encourage you to do things, you are wanting to take a break from or make changes.

Let's get something straight. This can be really hard and you have to be really firm and clear. When you are ready to start making changes, be clear about why you want to do them and what it will give you. Also, be clear about what you want to tell others.

You may want to just tell a close circle of friends what you are doing. I am taking some time off, I want to lose some weight, or there is something I am working on at work that needs my attention. Find something that works for you that you can use and have ready. It's even better if it is the real reason (obviously!). I want to get healthier so I am sorting my diet and exercise out.

This can be hard if the reason you are changing is because of something going wrong in your life. I don't suggest for one minute you air your dirty laundry, particularly if every time you talk about it, it makes you feel bad. Like my story things had been terribly wrong for some time and then got really bad. I didn't feel the need to share that with anyone other than my close friendship group. For a long time if I spoke about it I felt bad about it. The last thing I needed to do was revisit those feelings of guilt and shame.

I know quite a few people like this, please be aware of this one. Don't be forced into situations where you are having to explain yourself. Especially if it feels negative, making you feel bad with guilt and shame. It's not healthy for you at this stage to be revisiting these emotions, it's not healthy ever to revisit these feelings. If you are changing because things got bad or something has gone wrong, you don't have to share that with anyone apart from people you trust to support you with it.

Find the people you can count on to support you with this. It took my friends and family a long time to understand what I was doing. Be prepared to deal with this for a long time until people just get used to it.

When you are out with colleagues and friends, have something ready. When people buy rounds they always expect everyone to have an alcoholic drink. Be ready with your statement you feel happy with: I am watching my weight, I am taking medication, I am allergic, I am not buying rounds, I am driving, whatever it is, so then you just aren't participating.

If you go out for tea/coffee with friends/family/ work colleagues and you are avoiding sugar, be ready with what you want to purchase: herbal tea, water, black coffee, tea, stay away from the cake counter and be ready with the reason that you don't want the big gooey cake. I am not hungry is a good one, although for some bizarre reason people will still try and force it on you.

Environment is Important

When you start making changes initially it's good to get into a routine and make it easy on yourself. If its alcohol don't go to the pub, stay out of the drinks aisle in the supermarket, avoid social events for a bit. It's the same with diet: don't buy the rubbish food and don't go out for dinner unless you really have to. Stay away from the action. Make it easy on yourself.

If your thing is a drug, then this can be easier to avoid in the early days as it's not so in your face as much as alcohol and food. Unless you only have friends that take drugs, then it can be tough. You will need to find other people to be around, volunteering, evening classes, sports etc.

Think about the environment you are going to be in and the people you will be with when socialising.

Where are you going and with whom?

If the environment is difficult, are there people there that can help you with your goals? If the environment is difficult and there is no one there to help you, I would say avoid it in the early days and I know this isn't a popular view. But when you are really wanting to make changes, you are really motivated and you have stuff in place that's going well you don't want to ruin that. It can be really easy to slip up in these environments.

I always find this is a funny one when I am explaining this to people and I'm getting them to think through and plan what they will say and how they will deal with these situations. I feel ridiculous saying what I have to say. As I hope we reach a point soon where it's obvious. We want to support people to be healthier and why wouldn't we. But for some bizarre reason we don't, as a group of people we encourage each other to be unhealthy and make unhealthy choices.

When you start making changes, this can uncover all sorts of things with your friends and family, so be ready for this.

Now not everyone will be like this, some of you will be lucky and have great supportive friends and family, if this is the case great, this is going to be a lot easier for you.

If not find at least one person who will support you, as I don't expect you to live a life of a nun and it's good to have someone to talk to about these things. Even better if you can find a friend to make changes with together, supporting each other.

Ideally what you want is one person, that you can talk to. Someone who supports you with the positive things in your life. Someone that helps you make healthier choices, eat healthy food, drink less and can back you up.

Task

I challenge you to find someone.

Find a family member or friend that:

- Supports you making healthy choices.
- Actively encourages you.
- Is someone you can turn to when feeling weak.
- Who gets it.

If you really can't find someone there are some great forums and closed groups out there, here are a couple.

I run a closed Facebook group for support and accountability. For ladies only. Women Who Don't Drink, its for ladies who want to change their relationship with alcohol.

One year no beer has a website forum and a closed Facebook group. I have experience of the Facebook group and its very good and supportive.

There will be lots of others. Have a look and find one that works for you.

The Significant Other

Let's talk about husbands, wives, and partners. This can be really difficult for lots of reasons.

Let's start with the partner that wants you to make changes.

Sounds easy doesn't it? Well it can be. But sometimes what can happen is they want it their way and can be too prescriptive about how this happens. I have seen many relationships where one partner is disciplined and can make healthy choices without any issue and then the other partner just struggles with drink, food and/or drugs. What can happen is you can get into a difficult scenario where it is them giving you a hard time about making changes. This can make things worse as it may just add to you feeling bad about yourself.

Make changes because **you** want to. It has to come from you. Yes, you may be listening to concerns from family members, partners etc. that's great, but it's you that decides to change and why. A partner cannot force you to change, they might give ultimatums that help to focus you and then you might decide to change because the relationship is more important. But it's still you that makes the change.

Ideally you want a supportive partner that is understanding, says clearly what they want for themselves and allows you to make your own decisions. Sounds great doesn't it.

For instance, I would not choose to be in a relationship with someone that drinks regularly. I wouldn't mind if someone had

159

the occasional drink, but someone that binged at the weekend or drank regularly at home would be an issue for me. I wouldn't want to be around it for purely selfish reasons. That's my choice and I am able to communicate that clearly.

Then we have the partner that also likes to participate in drinking, smoking, eating junk food or maybe even taking recreational drugs. Maybe this is part of your relationship, something you do together. If you both want to make changes and can support each other in a positive way, great. However sometimes what can happen is that one person wants to make changes and the other doesn't and; it's entirely up to that person when they start and what they do. One of the worse things you can do is pressure someone to change, particularly in close relationships. It causes so much friction.

But there are ways of dealing with this appropriately so it doesn't come across as a pressure or a source of irritation within the relationship. **One of the most important things you can do is own what you say. Using "I" statements when talking about how you feel.**

I know you are probably thinking she has gone all therapy fluffy woo woo on me. But seriously there are a couple of things I picked up from my relationship training and this is one of them that I have used when working with couples and it really works, even if you feel silly to start off with. Even if you feel silly all the time saying "I" because you are not used to it. Do it, it works.

For example, say I am in a relationship with someone and I want to make changes but they don't. I really need them to encourage me, not discourage me. I am totally ok with them doing what they want but please don't actively try to get me to join in with them.

Say it's about alcohol (it could be anything). I make the decision to make changes, I need to for my health, my work, my children and I am feeling rubbish a lot and my life just isn't working for me. I make time to talk to my partner about this. Using "I" statements about my life: "I feel like I need to start reducing and stop drinking for a while", "I really want take a break", "I feel tired and sluggish all the time and just don't feel on top of things", "I know I could be doing so much more in my life so I really want to get a grip on this." "I would really like it if you supported me with this. You can support me by: not drinking around me, not buying alcohol and bringing it into the house, helping me when I say I want to have a drink, encourage me to keep going." What you are hoping for is a good response.

If the partner is going to struggle to be able to support you in this, because of their own bad habits and the need to keep them going, that's up to them. There is nothing you can do about this apart from express your disappointment. After all in a relationship you are a team, hopefully supporting each other in your lives. But it maybe that the other person is not able to make changes at this point.

It is still possible to make changes without your partner supporting you, but you will need to be strong and they will need to make sure they are not actively encouraging you. If they are and won't respect that you need to make changes, you really need to talk about this.

I have worked with a lot of couples where one wants to make changes and the other doesn't. I have found it very useful if each couple has a grown-up conversation using "I" statements and really listens to each other. So, don't give up trying to get them to hear you and support you. Sometimes change takes time, sometimes people need to see you making the change and then they support.

Ultimately you are still individuals with individual lives and choices, yes you are in a relationship and you need to consider each other but not at the expense of your health.

Remember actions speak louder than words. Over 70% of communication is non-verbal, so your partner may say one thing, but when it comes down to it they do support you with their actions. So try not to get too upset if the initial conversation doesn't go very well. Just get on with making changes for yourself anyway.

If you are in a relationship where someone buys you your alcohol, cigarettes, bad food or drugs this really needs to be tackled. If conversations don't go well I suggest you have a few sessions of couples counselling as there could be something else going on here. They need to stop doing this for you. If they don't it will be very difficult to make changes.

Sometimes people are well meaning and think they are being nice, like my dad always wanting to pour me a champagne cocktail. In his head he is being nice. He just doesn't get it. Luckily I don't have to live with it and I can choose when I visit; mostly anyway.

If you have a relationship, friendship or family bond that is based on any of these things and the other person is supportive it's about finding other things you can do together to replace this. If after work you and your partner share a bottle of wine or more, then what can you do together instead to unwind and talk about the day?

If this is the case, make a list together:

- What other things can you do?
- When can you start doing these other things?

It could be going for a walk after work, maybe walking home together or having date nights that don't include your bad habit. There are so many things you can do differently.

Maybe you smoke together or watch movies eating pizza and ice cream every night. Be ready, make a plan. If this is you as a couple, be really honest, your togetherness is based around doing things you want to change. Come up with things you can do that are good for you.

Change your habits and patterns together, but at your own pace. Encourage and support, don't make the other person wrong.

Wider family and friends is another thing altogether as you can actually mostly stay away from them if they are not supportive or even actively making it hard for you. I don't suggest for one minute you stay away from friends and family. But if you really want to make changes and you are very clear that what you have been doing has been having some impact on your life then you have to be realistic in the beginning, least for the first few months.

Spotlight on Drinking

A friend of mine who had a serious problem with alcohol, stopped for quite some time, years even. Then one day he decided he would drink again moderately. This didn't really work out for him as he struggles with moderation and alcohol is a biggy for him. He stopped again and made a conscious effort to do things differently rather than just stopping. He continued to go out with his friends, one night we were out together with a group of friends. Dancing and having a nice time, I wasn't drinking either and 1 hour in he said, "I have got to go". I asked him "why?" He said, "Being in a bar surrounded by alcohol isn't a good place for an alcoholic". Now I don't like the term alcoholic it has too many negative connotations and actually we are all different and our drinking patterns are different.

What we need to do to get help or stop or reduce are different, so it really isn't that simple. Yes, there are a small percentage of people who have serious drink problems: daily dependant drinkers, drinkers that need a detox, that are unable to reduce on their own. They probably need to not drink ever again, as they have probably damaged their emotional and physical health in some way, so why make it worse by drinking again. But my point is, for my friend it was easier to avoid the situation altogether at that stage.

It can be really hard when you first make that change. You don't even need to stop, maybe you just drink less or change your drinking. But let's face it, the first people to notice are your friends and family.

You would think you would just be able to make the change and no one notice, but oh no, we are a nation of drinkers (sorry I hate saying that, but it's true). And most are too quick to comment on the fact you are drinking a soft drink.

Ultimately, it's a no brainer for me, plain and simple. Alcohol is a highly toxic substance that effects the whole body. For some people it can have disastrous consequences and if someone chooses to take a break, prioritise their health or whatever their reasons this can be only a good thing, right? And they deserve the support of their loved ones and most people will support you.

If there is someone in your life that repeatedly makes it difficult for you maybe you need to have a serious conversation with them about this. I have always found snippets of facts, making it about me, not them, educating people very slowly and in short bursts, works.

Be true to yourself, stand firm, make it about you, accept them for who they are and don't judge. Do not lecture (that's the important bit if you keep it about you, people listen, if you make it about them and their drinking they may not).

A wonderful thing can happen (it does take time). People start asking questions in a positive way, being interested, learning from you and making changes themselves. You will even have people start to confide in you that have a problem with alcohol.

In my friendship group and family they are now very well educated about alcohol. They are all making an informed choice. Surely that's a good thing, right?

The Couple That Parties Together.

I have seen many couples that struggle with their relationship when one or both need to start making changes to their drinking, eating or even recreational party drug taking (whatever you want to call it).

If you have been together a long time and a big part of your relationship is social. You like to go out, you have a big group of friends, you all party together etc. This can be a massive part of your life, almost like a hobby. For some people it can be their reason for work. The old, work hard all week, play hard at the weekends. This all sounds really simple and to others it might sound simple to make changes. It's not and can be really hard for the relationship.

Richard and Diane's Story

Richard and Diane have been together over 20 years, they have children together. He works hard and is the main bread winner, he feels this responsibility, it's all on him. Bringing the money in, paying the bills, supporting everyone. For some people they really feel this and it can be quite a pressure at times. He lets off steam by drinking. Occasionally she worries about his health, the impact of his drinking. He knows its not a good idea for him to drink as much as he does but its his escape. A large part of their life is their socializing, their friends, fun, partying, they love it.

Then she decides she has had enough of all the partying and drinking and wants to make changes to her lifestyle, for herself. Life changes in a very short time, it's very clear she wants their lives to change. However she needs their lives to change it helps her if they are in it together, after all they have pretty much done everything else together. Because Richard doesn't want to change, and the only reason he needs to is because it would be supportive for her, (oh yes and good for his health but he isn't motivated by that) it becomes even more difficult for him. The pressure is on, for him to give up, it's unspoken.

This can be a very difficult situation in a relationship, particularly a long term one, there is so much invested in a way of life. Choice is big for people, we can't inflict our demands on others, even though we do. When we care for people we want them to make good choices, it can be the hardest thing in the world to accept people for who they are and what they are doing. But in this situation and many others like this we need to.

This applies to so many things you can't change other people. Listen, this one is really important, **YOU CAN'T CHANGE OTHER PEOPLE.**

You can accept the situation. Then the best thing you can do is work on yourself, make the changes you want to make, live life how you want to. Sometimes people get curious and follow you.

If you are close to anyone, wives, husbands, partners, children, friends, brothers sisters etc. the list goes on. You care for them, you want the best for them. But it is their life, you can be there, you can give advice, you can love unconditionally, but you can't change them.

Accept that you cannot change others, but you can change yourself, you are in charge of you.

Not everyone
will understand
your journey,
thats ok.

You're here to
live your life,
not to make everyone
understand.

unknown

11. Being a parent

If you are a mum or dad, all the other stuff I have written about making changes to improve YOUR life may seem a little out of reach. Particularly if you have little ones, are a single parent, your partner works a lot or you work as well or maybe all these.

However, I am going to call bullshit again.

There is always a reason why you can't do the things you need to do in your life to make it better.

This book is about habit, about health, about change and about clearing space so you can figure out what you need. It's the first bit you need to do to make changes.

Like I have said a few times, if you are not spending your time on your bad habits it frees you up for so much more.

If eating is your bad habit, it takes time to buy food, think about it pretty much all the time, give yourself a hard time about what you have eaten or not eaten and exercising to compensate. All these things take up so much time.

Drinking, buying alcohol, hangovers and generally not functioning at your best. This takes up more time than you realise.

If busyness is your vice, do less get more. Yes really, if you just do what you have to do, I mean really prioritise, after all your children don't remember things like mum/dad was so great they did the washing up. Then you can squeeze in a bit of time for you: relaxation, something fun, you will be surprised what happens in the space.

You miss things if you are busy.

Tired, I don't have to tell you this one, you really aren't functioning well at all.

The same with stress.

So, mums/dads, it's all the more important that you look after yourself. I have lost count of how many parents (I have to say this is mostly mums) I have worked with that haven't put themselves first sometimes. How can you be a good parent if you don't make some good choices for yourself?

I am not asking you to be supermum/dad, in fact I think that's half the problem. Stop giving yourself a hard time, (remember your self-imposed to do list) and spend time working on your bad habits. You will feel so much better and this will make life a lot easier in so many ways.

The other bit about parenting is the role modelling. If you decide to make healthy choices for your life, your children see that, they learn it. As a parent we all want what is best for our children, we want them to be happy, healthy.

What better way for them to learn that, but from you. It's not fool proof as you know, but it's a start.

If you learn about your drinking, eating and make better choices and live a healthier life, that impacts on them. Your children learn this. If you make time for exercise, leisure activities, fun, your children learn this. If you work less, or change your job to one that makes you happier, they learn that they can do work, they enjoy.

Remember what you want for your children, what are you showing them with the way you live your life?

Now don't give yourself a hard time, you are not perfect, people aren't perfect. What can you do to make changes today?

Over to You

I want you to think about your bad habit.

- If you make changes what do you gain?
- If you're bad habit where to disappear when you woke up tomorrow. What would you see, hear and feel?
- How would you know it had disappeared? Write it down now.
- What are the benefits to you prioritising, changing your bad habits?
- The benefits to you?
- The benefits to the children?
- The benefits to your partner?

- If you don't have a partner how does that change what type of relationship you would like to have?

Guilt and shame.

When I have worked with mums/dads to change habits, sometimes what's stopping them is the guilt of situations in the past when they don't think they have been the best parent they can be.

It's in the past, you can't change it, but you can change your here and now.

What can you do?

There is nothing to be gained from focussing on the past. No-one gains from it.

It depends what has happened in the past, but sometimes our children can give us a hard time, just when we don't need it. Here is the thing. If they do, the chances are they would have given you a hard time anyway. That's their job, particularly teenagers. Its ok, when they are giving you grief it doesn't mean they don't love you. So if you are someone that feels like you have made a few mistakes in your past and this has impacted on your children. Do what you need to do to make it better, make sure you don't stay in that past emotion, event,

it doesn't service anyone to stay in the guilt and shame attached to this.

Like I said, you can't change the past. All you can do is show people you have changed. Actions speak louder than words. My eldest son loved to give me a hard time for quite some time. I let him have his say, we talked about it, I was honest, then enough was enough. I asked him, "do you think I have changed?" And he said "yes" and that was it end of the conversation, for me anyway, not for him.

Show people you are different, that you want your life to be different. You can have all the conversations in the world, actions speak louder than words.

Never regret anything that has
happened in your life,
it cannot be changed,
undone or forgotten.
So take it as a lesson learned
and move on.

Unknown

12. Exercise

As we have all heard a million times, exercise is important for so many things.

It's important for our physical health – as long as we don't overdo it. And really important for our emotional health.

Even if all you do is go for a walk 30 minutes a day. It doesn't have to be anything amazing. You can even think about how you can build that into your normal day so it isn't an extra thing you need to do.

One of the things I have noticed is if people are interested in exercise when they start making time for this it reduces the time they spend on their bad habits. Then they start making more changes as they want to be able to do more exercise. The more they do it, the more they enjoy it, the easier it becomes to make changes in other areas.

I once worked with a lady who had been drinking, quite a lot; 2 bottles of wine a day. Life had got difficult like it does. Divorce, children, money, work, difficult relationships. It had all just started to stack up. She started running to help a friend, mostly because she needed to do something. She knew that, but didn't know what to do. It was as simple as a friend asking her to help her. She started to run a couple of times a week. Building up her distance. What happened was that when she was running the next day she didn't want to be hungover so she could run better and get the most out of it. She started to feel the endorphin rush you can get from exercise.

It stopped being a thing that she actively had to force herself to do and started becoming a good habit.

The friend then suggested they do some events starting with 5k. They did a few 5k events and found that having something to train for really helped their running. Then they started doing 10k events. This went on until they started doing tri-athlons. So then came the swimming and cycling training.

Before she knew it, naturally she had built up her training schedule and the drinking just fell away. Because life was difficult she needed something healthy, something that was good for her that she could immerse herself in.

Starting this really simple thing, helping a friend, turned into the thing that significantly turned around her bad habits, physical and emotional health. Slowly and steadily without actively focussing on the thing she wanted to change.

It also fitted in with her life. Things she could do in 1 hour, worked with the children and her work.

It was a gift without her even realising it.

I call this making changes around the back door. Sometimes actually focusing on the thing you want to change doesn't help. Sometimes it better to pick something you can do that's good for you. Something that fits in with your life that you can't do if you are doing your bad habit. So naturally things change.

If exercise was a pill it would be our most beneficial.

I want you to read that again and again. How amazing is that, something you can do daily, for free even, that helps you to feel good and improves your physical health.

I talk about exercise in all my on-line programmes and my 1-1 work, if I could I would get every doctor to prescribe it, with sleep, 3 healthy meals a day and 2ltrs of water.

Exercise significantly reduces our risk of heart disease, stroke, type 2 diabetes, cancer by 50%. Lowering our risk of early death by 30%. Now alcohol increases our risk of all of these things. That doesn't mean you can drink and exercise and the 2 cancel each other out, doesn't work like that. Take a break from drinking and start exercising. If health isn't a big motivator for you, just the release of endorphins should be enough.

Now you might say I can't run, or swim or cycle, or I am too overweight. There are a number of excuses I am sure you have ready. I don't have time, blah blah blah.

It can be anything that's good for you that doesn't take up too much of your time: a dance class?

You can even start with 10 minutes a day walking. If you feel self-conscious and you don't want to go to a gym or exercise outside, around people, there are so many workout videos on you tube or little workout apps.

Something that you can't do if you are drinking, hungover, wasted.

Pick a few things you could do and make a list of realistic and achievable ideas.

There is no point putting something down if you know you won't do it in a million years.

When you have 5 things on your list and you are honest and can say that yes you can do those things, you can make space for them in your life.

Scale them 0-5. 5 being the most interesting for you and 0 not interested and start with the one that you score the highest

Book time in to do it, make it happen, no matter what. Trust me there will always be something, a reason not to do it. If you enjoy it, book time in regularly to do it again whatever it is. Until it becomes a habit.

Food is the most abused anxiety drug.
Exercise is the most underutilised anti depressant.

Bill Phillips

13. Dealing with difficult thoughts – its all in the mind

Some of us have a lot of negative self-talk, negative thoughts going around our heads. Usually what happens is throughout the day you can be saying negative things to yourself about different things that happen throughout the day.

I have noticed this with a lot of people. There are several different things that happen.

It could be that you have negative self-talk.

Don't worry about this it doesn't mean you're mad. A lot of people do it, it's part of your process, how you think, how you process information.

It might be that your thoughts are negative about lots of different things.

Negative thoughts take up a lot of energy and what we think, effects how we feel, which effects how we behave. This isn't something you are consciously aware of. You may not even be aware of your thoughts.

The good news is you can learn to change it.

Emotions are things we feel throughout the day. They are usually short lived, based on thoughts we have, interactions with other people and the things we are doing.

Emotions are also likely to have a definite and identifiable cause. For example, after disagreeing with a friend over politics, you might feel angry for a short period of time.

A mood on the other hand is usually much milder than an emotion, but longer-lasting. In many cases, it can be difficult to identify the specific cause of a mood. For example, you might find yourself feeling gloomy for several days without any clearly identifiable reason.

The good news is we don't have to be a slave to emotions or moods, we can get ourselves out of different negative moods if we choose to.

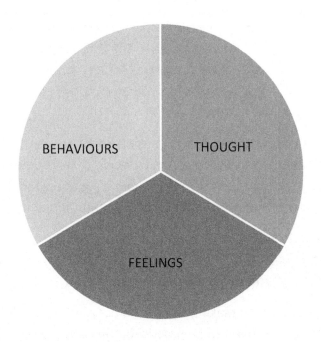

Thoughts – Internal thoughts – Dialogue – speaking inside your head.

Feelings – Emotions – Internal state – how we feel inside.

Behaviour – Actions, words – What we do.

I want you to take on board that we will feel different emotions throughout any day.

The one thing I can guarantee you is they will change, you are unlikely to feel the same emotion all day. So, start noticing your emotions, just be aware of them and don't act on them.

The diagram above illustrates that; what we think - effects how we feel - effects how we behave. The three are interchangeable. Now I know this sounds obvious and common sense but you would be surprised how many people are not actually aware of this.

For instance, something happens at work that you then feel angry about, because of this you decide to have a drink. Because you feel angry you end up having a few too many. You go home to your partner and have an argument.

All this started with something happening at work, then reacting to this emotion by drinking, which then made the feeling and your behaviour harder to control.

Now I know I am making this sound easy, but again this is another good habit to be practiced, the more you do it, the easier it becomes. Start noticing what you do around this, noticing your process, what is happening? When you feel a negative emotion, what just happened?

Words and meaning.

Let's get something straight words are just words, we choose to give them meaning.

Throughout your day many people will say and do many different things.

How this affects you is entirely up to you.

You have a **response-ability.**

Now I am not suggesting you behave like a robot, after all we are only human. So someone will do or say something and you will notice your emotional response to this, you can choose to stay in this emotion or alternatively, if it is a negative one you can deal with it similar to dipping your toe in a hot bath. In and out!! Shake it off.

Why would you choose to stay in a negative emotion?? Why would you choose to allow yourself to feel bad??

For example –

Someone close to you is having a difficult time, could be a child, teenager, partner anyone. Take the teenager that is under pressure during their exam year.

They have a busy social life, school is tough, on top of that they have lots of course work to do. It's all getting a bit real. Some teenagers struggle at the best of times, all those hormones and growing up, let alone put something in there that actually is difficult. They are moody, difficult, shouting lots and generally giving you a hard time. As a parent it can be tough to be around, especially if it's all the time and the behaviour and arguments get out of control sometimes. Emotionally you can feel drained. The best thing to do here is be objective and understanding, joining them in the emotion and the drama is not going to help the situation. You can choose how you respond, you have a response-ability. If you make the interaction, situation, mean things about your parenting, take whatever they say personally, you get emotionally involved, upset and angry, it only perpetuates the whole thing for the family. Whereas if you can accept that's it's just them having a difficult time, be there, love them, help in some way. Trust me it will feel a lot nicer for all concerned, if you can be at cause rather than effect.

Notice during your interactions with people what happens with your emotions, be present. If you start to feel bad for any reason, what just happened?

Did you make it mean something?

Did you assume?

We are not mind readers. People like to tell me often that they know what people are thinking and obviously they don't.

Mostly people aren't thinking about them. Although I have spent most of this book asking you to make time for you, **it's actually not all about you.**

Sometimes people spend time thinking about what they think others are thinking about them. (Hope you followed that.) So basically guessing, worrying what others are thinking about. 9 x out of 10 they are not thinking about you, well not in the way you think.

Very rarely are people thinking what you think they are thinking about.

Unless you ask them you just don't know. One of the best things you can do is accept this, take this on board. It really frees you up.

What is going on in your body
impacts your mind and emotions.
And what is going on
in your mind and emotions
impacts on your physical body.

We get what we focus on, so focus on what you want!!!

Your focus (your thoughts) produce behaviour based on what you are focussing on.

So, for instance,

If you think about food a lot, inevitably you will be eating a lot.

If all you can think about is having a glass of wine when you get home, the first thing you are going to do when you get home is have some wine.

I think about chocolate in the afternoon at work, I think about it, I make a picture of it, I start thinking about what it tastes like, then I start salivating. All I need then is someone to go to the shop and get me some. I focus on chocolate then I want it.

This is one of the reasons diets don't work for some people. They are spending their time focusing on what they can't have so of course they are going to have it.

Very simple, but I am sure you get the idea.

Focus on what you want. Not what you don't want.

Pay attention to your thoughts.

If you find yourself thinking thoughts you don't want, change your focus.

What can you do to change it?

So, you know what you don't want.......

What do you want instead?

Your focus is what produces results in your life.

For example, the young mum who decides she will be the best mum she can be, spends her time reading about parenting, befriending other parents and asking questions so she can learn from them, maybe even attending parenting classes. She is spending her time focusing on being the best parent she can be. She may not be perfect but you can bet eventually she will be doing a good job and feeling better about herself as a parent.

When you want to lose weight and you are a massive sugar eater, you might be saying to yourself, I can't have that, I can't have this etc. You are focusing on what you can't have, that's going to be hard. Instead, try saying I can eat this, then focus on what you can have, what are healthy choices for you?

You want to start making changes with your drinking. If you are focusing on not drinking, you are still thinking about drinking making it hard for yourself. You could focus on doing something different, like exercise, playing with the kids, going to the cinema, you get the idea by now.

Ok, so you may tell me I don't know what I want.

Don't worry, we can do some work on this:

Over to You

- Make a note of the things you spend your time doing and thinking, sometimes it helps to look at it on paper, and mostly we know anyway.
- Then write what you would rather be spending your time doing and thinking.

It could look something like this –

I spend my time thinking about negative things, how I am over weight, or I don't like the way I look. I give myself a hard time about not being a good enough mum. I really struggle at work as well, I think people don't like me. I am tired, I drink every night and eat a lot of rubbish, at the weekends I am just catching up with washing, ironing and the kids.

I would like to feel good about myself, feel healthy, lighter. I want to have the energy to spend time with the kids. Maybe if I felt better about myself I would find it easier to socialize at work.

With the 2nd paragraph, she says how she wants to be, feel, next its looking at what she needs to be doing for this to happen.

Actions might be –

- Take a break from drinking – lose weight, sleep better, have more energy, improve self-esteem.

- Eat healthy foods – lose weight, sleep better, have more energy, feel better about myself.
- Do an activity with the kids at the weekend – exercise is good for my mental health, lose weight, feel better, improve self-esteem, feel better as a mother, role modelling.
- Walk to work – exercise, reduce stress, feel better, improve self-esteem.

Focussing on what she can do will help, but the key here is to also pay attention to the thoughts around it. Be clear about why you are doing it and what the benefits are. The chances are you will be more focussed in your mind.

This may seem simple but sometimes we don't realise what we want until we take a moment to focus on it.

Lilly's story

I first met Lilly some time ago. She had got herself into a spot of bother without realising it. Using drugs, drinking, getting involved with people she didn't want to and getting into debt. She really wasn't looking after herself. She started as a teenager, again unconsciously making choices to help her escape as things weren't working out for her and she wasn't really paying attention. She was a teenager and like a lot of us if things go wrong when we are teenagers unless we get lucky or there is someone there to pick us up and keep looking out for us it can continue into adulthood.

So it had started out as what most people would call teenage experimenting. But when we started to work together it was clear it was an escape.

Then her sister died suddenly in her mid-20's. This was very difficult for her to deal with. And this is when she got into trouble. Initially we worked together so she could stop her damaging habits and patterns, which she did. She learnt techniques and put things in place to help her. She changed her life completely and moved on very quickly.

Life was good. She had a new partner, was very much in love, her education was going well, had a good job, lots of traveling and great supportive friends. But she noticed that sometimes things went wrong and she didn't really understand why. Self-sabotage she called it.

As we worked together again it became very clear that she was struggling with anxiety daily. What she was thinking was affecting her thoughts, how she felt and then her behaviour.

There was a lot of negative insecure self-talk, questioning every interaction she had. Was that ok? Did she say the right thing? Do they like me? She was getting too caught up in thinking about what people thought about her. That in turn effected how she felt, that horrible, anxious, squirmy feeling. This would dictate how she reacted to these situations that mostly didn't even warrant a reaction at all. Other people wouldn't have noticed what happened for Lilly.

After sorting out her initial problem with taking drugs and drinking, then the euphoria of a new life and everything working out so well. She then began to notice what was underneath it all.

The creation of the problem.

For Lilly this was a hangover from a childhood that was good in parts. She was loved, fed cared for, educated etc. However it was lacking in other parts. There were a number of situations that had quite appropriately created fear in her as a child which had then turned into insecurity, feeling not worthy and anxiety as an adult.

This kind of thing is hard to figure out when you are using, as you are too busy coming up and down.

Once the dust settles sometimes if we are lucky we can see the pattern. Lilly could see that something wasn't working for her. Then she was brave enough to ask for help.

After taking part in some coaching she learned how to have a better response to these situations and feels a lot better about herself as an adult. Her world is her oyster.

How she thought about herself affected how she felt, which affected her behaviour which caused her problems in her relationships in turn making her feel sad. She sought help and now feels very different.

YOUR MIND IS A GARDEN
YOUR THOUGHTS ARE THE SEEDS
you can grow flowers
OR YOU CAN GROW WEEDS

15. What happy healthy people do.

Its really simple actually. They keep it simple. The don't sweat the small stuff. They have a good perspective on life, they are grateful.

They don't hang onto past resentments.

They don't over analyse.

They don't make things mean things.

They don't spend time worrying about what may or may not happen, things they have no control over.

They focus on what they have, rather than what they havnt got.

They don't compare themselves to others, because they know we are all different.

They don't complain, they know that there is always someone worse off.

They know what is important, which is actually very little.

My advice to you is to keep things as simple as you can. If you find you world getting small and you are making small things big. Then get some perspective, expand your horizons, spend time with different people, volunteer, anything that gets you out of your head and world.

16. If what you are doing isn't working do something different

This is so key and so obvious when you really spend time to think about it.

If you do what you have always done………….

You will get what you have always got!!!

Sounds obvious doesn't it, now really take some time to think about this sentence.
If what you are doing isn't working, do something different.
It doesn't say try, it says do.
Then you keep doing things different until you find something that works.
Obviously, you give the new thing a chance.
It doesn't always work on the first attempt, maybe even, second or third. Persist.

You would be surprised at the amount of people I speak to who are doing things they don't want to do any more. Or maybe they want their life to be different but they just can't figure out how to get there.

I love these little sayings, they are so simple and clear.

The definition of insanity is doing the same thing and expecting a different result.

It's quite simple really TAKE ACTION. Do something different no matter how small and then keep doing the different thing until things start to change. The rule here is that the new habit you choose needs to be

- Something you enjoy!
- Feels good when you do it
- Is healthy – good for you – remember we are changing the bad habits
- Supports your future

When you make a choice or a decision that effects your life ask yourself "does this support my current plan for the future?"

This is a big one write this down and remember it and use it throughout the day, be specific with your goal.

Keep asking yourself the question. "Does this support my goal of............?

For example, the middle-aged woman who wants to lose weight, if every time she goes to buy, cook or eat some food she asks herself "how does this support my goal of getting into my favourites dress for the party in a month?" or even "losing a few pounds and feeling healthier and fitter".

A young man who is staying at home and using cannabis, unhappy in his work and life, wants to go travelling and meet a lovely lady. If he continues staying at home smoking weed the chances are nothing will change. If he asks himself everyday "is what I am doing now helping me to save money

To go travelling? "

The woman who is tired, stressed, overweight, drinks, eats too much, is too tired to exercise, doesn't have the energy to do anything, cries a lot, complains to her friends about her life etc. Unless she does something nothing will change. Sometimes it can feel overwhelming, how she can possibly find time to exercise or the energy even. Its chicken and egg, she is so tired she eats rubbish, so stressed she uses alcohol to relax at the end of the evening, which affects her sleep, making her feel more tired, it's also empty calories adding to her weight and general feeling of unhealthy ness. Too tired to eat healthy foods, too tired to exercise.

Unless she does something different nothing will change, so what can she do that will help herself to start making changes? Work less for a while? Change her job? Take some time off to kick start the new habits? Take some time off to sleep, then start eating healthy, then start exercising small bits at a time, then work out a new routine so she doesn't get into the same mess. Ultimately if she is tired due to work, it means working less or changing the job.

If she doesn't make a change at some point there will be a crash, whether it's in 6 months, a year or longer there will be one.

> "The definition of insanity, is doing the same thing and expecting a different result."

Albert Einstein

17. How to start, How to make small changes, small changes, small steps.

Throughout this book, on pretty much every page there are so many ways you can make changes and tips to get started. All it takes is one thing, one small thing, and then another and so on until you get to where you want to go.

Doing the drink diary, food diary, 10 minutes' exercise, going to bed earlier, relaxing for a bit everyday, doing a new hobby, walking to work instead of driving, spending 30 minutes a day looking for a new job, do that training course you have always wanted to do. The list is endless, all the above are in this book and I am sure there are many that aren't.

The point is pick something and start.

Action is so important, stop thinking about what your life could be like, make it happen.

Only you can do this.

There is no Knight in shining armour, no fairy godmother, no one is coming to save you.

But here's the good news you can save yourself as you have heard me say a million times already.

For some people their life has got so out of control they need to make the big change and that's ok if that's what they need to do. For others its making small changes that add up to the way you want your life to be.

Keep doing different things until you find the things that work for you.

For some people saving the money they would have spent on their alcohol can be really powerful. Putting it in a pot, making sure the pot has on it what you are going to do with the money a picture or something. Say it's a holiday, whatever motivates you.

I can remember a conversation I had with a young mum who wanted to give up smoking. She was talking to me about holidays. She really wanted to take her family on holiday but just couldn't afford it. We talked about her smoking, how much her and her partner smoke, and how much they both really want to give up for health reasons. We added up how much they were spending between them, it came to £5000 per year. Now that's one great family holiday right there, even 2 (She had 5 children so it was going to be expensive). She was horrified as she had not thought of her smoking in financial terms. She started on a smoking cessation programme, patches, texts, and groups and put the money away in a pot with a picture of her holiday on it. She found this way more motivating than all the other health reasons that we know about, but we can't see them, so for some reason they don't apply to us. I know that's silly right but it's true.

There is something about seeing it, knowing it, making the impact concrete in our heads to help the motivation. Like when you eat a chocolate bar you don't see it go on your hips. Or the alcohol you drink you don't see what its doing to your stomach, or liver. But the money in a pot you can see add up.

You can count it every week and feel good about all the money you have saved and be thinking about what you are going to do with it.

It's the same with alcohol, we know (well hopefully you do) its damaging for our health over the long-term. However we can't see it so it's not a motivator. You have to find something that is current for you now, that motivates you.

How to Start Stopping

Here is the thing: Just start.

Maybe you are someone that needs to plan for it, that's fine. Don't make the start date too long in advance. I get that sometimes you have to get your ducks lined up.

However be careful you are not making excuses, if you want to do this, just do it.

If you are drinking a lot daily and need to reduce, you may need to see a medical professional first anyway.

Maybe you need a medically assisted detox or reduction plan. This is part of the planning for it.

If you are daily dependant drinker or using a substance that is physically addictive (Opiates, benzos) then you need to work with a medical professional on reduction and planning.

Follow the tips in this book, and just start, plan if you have to, be clear about why you are doing it and find what motivates you, to help you stay on track.

EVERY DAY
IS A NEW DAY.

ITS NEVER
TOO LATE
TO START AGAIN.

18. What to do if you slip up

Now people don't like talking about this one, but we need to. Whatever you are changing, giving up or if you are just making healthier choices there will be times when: you have the cigarette, the drink, drink too much, don't go to the gym or the evening class that's helping you, eat too much of the wrong thing etc.

It's ok.

We are not perfect and life isn't perfect.

Very few people actually give up something and then never do it again.

Abstinence, for some people is the only way, but not for others.

Also, it maybe that you need to abstain from some things and not others.

Only you will be able to figure this out.

Even people who are incredible healthy, healthy eaters, people who exercise a lot, nutritionists etc. eat ice cream from time to time, or have a take away, chips, the odd glass of champagne.

People call these events relapses, slips, going backwards etc. Lots of horrible negative words that make us feel bad.

I once worked with a young lady who was an excessive binge drinker, really putting herself at risk physically and emotionally. She wanted to stop, for her life to be different.

She did ok, put things in place to really help herself. She went out one day with a friend and found herself at the bar and bought a glass of wine. Once she sat down and started drinking it she realised what she was doing. She drank the wine and stopped there. She felt really bad and gave herself a hard time. Really though it was a success since she was a binge drinker, someone who can't stop once they start. She realised what she was doing and stopped herself.

The language you use is very important, it needs to work for you.

Let's start with the language you use for stopping. You can call it reducing, gaining some control, moderating, if that works for you that's ok. You could also just want to stop for a while, take a break.

More often than not I see and hear people being very negative about slipups. There are lots of reasons for this. If you have set yourself a challenge, say 3 months off the booze and you have a drink 6 weeks in you can feel quite disappointed in yourself. Also maybe the drink didn't taste very nice, you drank too much and you feel horrible. You have a hangover or are un-well etc.

Stop right there, don't dwell in the negative. When this happens I usually see and hear people giving themselves a hard time, focusing on the bad: why did I do that? I feel terrible, what a waste, now I have to start again etc. etc.

It's in the past you can't change it, so there is no point giving yourself a hard time. However, what you can do is look at it objectively.

Task

1 or 2 days after you have a blip, no later. Sit down with a pen and paper, if you need to get an objective realistic friend to help. And think about:

- What happened?
- Why did you have a drink?
- Did you just want to?
- Were you craving one?
- Was it as simple as that you were around it and eventually you gave in?
- Did people pressure you?
- Have you had a bad day?
- Have you had a good day?
- Were you rewarding yourself?

The list of reasons goes on and on.

The point of this exercise is to be clear in a rational objective way (no beating yourself up!)

Sometimes there isn't a reason, it's as simple as you where there and alcohol/the thing was put in front of you and you thought why not? Or it's just a habit with those people.

At work when you work on a project, you have a plan that is time framed, with jobs allocated to different people and someone managing the project. During the project and at the end there is a constant review process. What is happening? Are things going according to plan? If not, why not? What can you do to get things back on track? What is needed to make it easier? Maybe there needs to be a change in plan? At the end, what worked? What didn't work? What can we do better next time? Learnings etc.

Why don't you do this with yourself? Be more objective about what you are doing?

My Journey with Alcohol

Some people like to set a time frame for reducing or stopping alcohol use. Again, find what feels right for you. For me, I just said I don't want to drink anymore, I stopped for quite some time, I can't remember how long. The time frame wasn't important to me, it still isn't. What was important was that I felt better, healthier and made better choices in my life because I wasn't drinking. I was very clear in my head I wasn't going to drink for these reasons.

I didn't say I was abstinent, I hadn't thought through if I would drink again, it wasn't important to me. All that mattered was that I wasn't drinking, that day, that week, that month and that

I felt better in myself. The more I didn't drink, the better I felt, the easier my life became, it became easier to deal with the difficult things in my life.

I started to get off on being sober, and having a clear head, the clarity of thought was amazing. The new habit grew from there.

My plan was to be healthy, make better choices, be a better parent and improve my life.

It worked for me, because I figured out how my brain works and what language to use for myself.

It's the same with food for me, if I say I can't have chocolate for a week, I guarantee you, I will be out down the shop buying a chocolate buffet. Whereas if I say to myself: "I am going to make healthy choices about what I put in my body" that works much better FOR ME. That's the crucial bit, figuring out what works for you. Everyone has an opinion, sometimes people get really militant about it, my way is the only way. But they are forgetting that we are not all the same.

I have worked with other people that drink regularly that are horrified at the thought of us focusing on reducing their drinking. We have had to go around the back door. What isn't working in their life? What do they want to change? How do they want things to be? We work on that and naturally as things improve the drinking reduces.

Also there are some people who come to support groups to help them stop drinking, the focus is on alcohol and then, because they are focusing on it, they want a drink.

Everyone is different.

I can remember one of my first blips clearly. My youngest has always been challenging with his behaviour, particularly with me. There are many reasons for this. We were on holiday and it was very tough. Emotionally challenging shall we say. I drank there because it was cheap (see what I did there). Then I came home and it was my birthday so I went out for lunch with friends. The week had been so horrendous I started drinking at 11am with friends and just continued throughout the day.

Let's just say things escalated and didn't end very well.

I woke up the next day and felt terrible physically and emotionally. Doing the classic "what did I do?" and "what did I say?" in my head, reliving the whole experience. The guilt and shame was phenomenal, excruciating.

I called a friend who was very supportive of me and knew what I was doing. He put me straight. Ok you had a blip, learn from it, move on, stop feeling sorry for yourself and get back on track. Give yourself the day in bed then call an end to it. He helped me nip it in the bud. No messing around.

I did, I dusted myself down and got back on track. No problem, I felt better in a few days.

Then I assessed what had happened. I was tired, in difficult situation with the youngest child, it was emotionally challenging and I was struggling with the whole situation. They were my triggers, so I needed to watch out for them.

There are so many reasons why you have a blip. And each time it can be different. You could be tired, stressed out, rewarding yourself, celebrating, being around certain friends or certain places etc.

And remember there doesn't have to be a cause. Sometimes there isn't a reason, its ok, it just is, you just did. So don't worry if you can't find a reason.

I had a rule, if I have been craving alcohol for whatever reason, I can't drink, I can't give into the craving, I have to sit with the craving and let it pass. It always passed and I survived and I felt 100% better than if I had given into it.

What to do if you slip up.

The best thing to do here is to just start again. Don't make a big deal out of it, don't get stuck in negativity, giving yourself a hard time.

Start again the next day when you wake up. And within 2 days:

Task

Sit down somewhere quiet, get a piece of paper and write down from the beginning, almost just before the beginning what happened when you slipped up.

It will look something like this.

"Normal day at work, quite busy, tired from a busy weekend with the kids. It's a friend's birthday and everyone is going to the local bar after work for a drink and some food. Sounds ok as there is food involved. I haven't had a drink for 6 weeks so I am feeling good and strong for my 3 month goal, all on track. I haven't really told my work friends what I am doing as there is a big drinking culture there and I just don't want to get into it. Also it's easy for me to avoid because I have children, I can just say I have to go, to get home. We go to the bar, I am ready to order my lime and soda, when my manager hands me a glass of wine. He has already been to the bar and got a round in for everyone, he is very generous like that. And I haven't told him, so why would he know. I don't want to say anything, so I stand there with it in my hand. I drink half of it, just because it's there. Then I leave and go home."

Simply writing it out, enables you to get better at understanding what happens. How simple it is and how easy it is to be in a situation doing the thing you don't want to. We seem to have this thing that we don't speak up, or we don't want to tell people. In this situation it's easy to look back and stop at the point where the manager gives you the wine and say, "thanks very much but I am not drinking at the mo" and getting yourself a soft drink. Job done, no big deal. Or even just putting it down and getting a water.

The other one to watch out for is the - in for a penny in for a pound thinking, "I have blown it so I might as well really go for it and enjoy it. "

NO! Stop! The "I have had a bite of the cake, so I am going to eat the whole cake." Believe me I have been there. Quit while you are ahead. Just stop as soon as you can.

So, if you have a drink, a bucket of takeaway chicken or whatever your poison is, just stop there.

Start again the next day, unpick it when you are not giving yourself a hard time.

If you have just done a period of time where you haven't participated in the thing you are stopping, great, feel good about that. Don't focus on the moment, the bit where it didn't go according to plan. Say you did 30 days, awesome, then one blip. Really you are going to let one blip get you down. 30 days is fab when you are starting to make changes.

I worked with a young lady in her 20's, she had a great job she loved and was doing really well. But she had got herself into a bit of trouble with alcohol and cocaine. It had started off with the normal partying and escalated. She was living in a big city with a high-pressured job, all the clichés I know. Her life had gone off on a tangent somewhere she had found herself in a place she didn't want to be. She knew what she wanted, good job, nice home, partner she loved, travel a bit, she had a plan. She felt good about this plan the only thing stopping her was, herself and the drinking and cocaine use. Cocaine is quite expensive so if you start using regularly it's not unusual to be spending more than £200 a week if not more. This soon adds up. Not only that, how you feel adds up, the come-downs, stress, using cocaine heavily, adds a whole other difficult dimension to your mental health and a busy life. She really wanted to stop, she worked really hard at it. It was tough because she was surrounded by the party lifestyle. We stripped back her life. What's working? What isn't working? She was struggling to stop and stay stopped because of it being around her. She changed her surroundings, where she worked and where she lived. She was really committed to changing. Immediately, she felt much better and it was easier to stay stopped. I remember early on when she managed one week, which was brilliant, as there had been a few difficult starts. Within a 2-week period she had used once, she had found herself in the wrong place, she was offered a drink and some cocaine and wasn't thinking, she took some, then she realised straight away. She left and went home; damage limitation. She really gave herself a hard time. We worked together to look at the positives, I think there was 2 weeks at this point, with one blip. She learnt from it and moved on. She went on to stay stopped and feel better week on week. If you have used anything regularly, after a few weeks of abstaining you really notice how much better you feel in yourself.

Every day is a new day and all that, cheesy I know, but it's true.

This is a real common thing. You are doing well. A slip up happens, then you focus on the slip up give yourself a hard time and stay in the negative which feels horrible.

And as we know, what we think effects how we feel, which effects our behaviour. In my sessions when this happens we spend quite a bit of time letting this one go.

"It's in the past you can't change it, in the here and now you aren't using. The plan is to not use today. You probably won't, so what can you do to take your mind off it and be nice to yourself to day?"

DAMAGE   LIMITATION
IF YOU START AGAIN
STOP.

Failure and feedback

A mindset I use in many areas in my life and I encourage all my clients to do so is: **there is no failure only feedback.** Failure is a loaded word, again, very negative. We learn by making mis-takes. If we go through life not making any mis-takes or getting anything wrong, how do we learn?

So, do your best to really take this on board. It may be that you make mis-takes in other areas of your life. Like parenting, work, sport, exercise, friendships, relationships etc. and you just reassess and learn from it. So, practice this in an area that's easier for you then transfer it. No one is perfect, we learn by making mis-takes as long as we don't stay in the negative feeling and beat ourselves up.

Mis- takes, when it doesn't work the first time, so you learn from it and move on. This is how we learn. I don't know about you, but I want to keep learning.

There is
no failure,
only
Feedback.

Robert Allen

19. Triggers & Cravings/urges

Everyone has cravings, everyone has different triggers and those triggers change depending on what is going on in your life.

Most people have cravings daily for many different things and our processes around that will be different.

It's getting to learn what yours are.

It's ok, to have cravings, I hear and see people talking about their cravings a lot as if it's something to be concerned about. "I am still having cravings 3 months in" I expect you will have them forever. It's normal. Your cravings will probably not disappear you will just get better at dealing with them.

The important thing is to not react to them.

It's the same as difficult emotions. When we talked about emotions before, remember you will experience a range of emotions throughout the day. And they pass, you don't act on all your difficult emotions? Well I hope not and if you do, go back to the emotions chapter and start doing some work. If you are a slave to your emotions, you may benefit from some extra coaching.

You may experience cravings: because you are tired, because you are stressed, because life is difficult, something bad just happened, habit and many more reasons. It doesn't have to be something negative that triggers them, it could be good things like celebrations, rewarding yourself, you just got the promotion etc. There might not even be a reason for them, they just happen.

There are a million and one things that happen, in our day, that can trigger cravings and then there are the things we are just used to, that we don't even think about. The unconscious things ingrained in our collective psyche. Cultural norms about certain types of behaviour, events, people and places. Before we even start talking about cravings that just pop up. There are the cravings that happen because you are in a certain place doing a certain thing, with certain people, the cultural and social stuff.

Weddings, stag and hen dos, birthdays, when a child is born, wetting the baby's head, parties, any celebration let's be honest, when you get that promotion, sealing a deal, Christmas, holidays, bank holidays and on and on. There are so many situations where for most of us it is ingrained in our psyche to associate them with alcohol, food, maybe even drugs.

To be at any of these events, around people indulging in drinking/using drugs etc. when you are actively making an effort to make healthy choices for your life can be very hard. You may very possibly experience cravings at these times. Quite simply because subconsciously it's somewhere where we would normally drink, or eat a certain food, take a drug.

Rubbishy, junky, sugary food has always been a big temptation for me. Even though I know it's rubbish and there is nothing of any use in there for me. It's something that I have to actively work with a lot. Christmas some years has been a huge worry. All that food and treats, people bring in chocolate and cake to work and giving it to you by the bucket load. It starts in early December and if you are like me you can be still dealing with your Christmas eating in April!

A lot of us are think in a very visual way, when we think, we visualize things, and we make pictures in our mind. For instance – **don't think about pink elephants**, the majority of you will be thinking about pink elephants now.

Visual triggers (just seeing the thing that you have been avoiding) can trigger a craving, as well as being around people that are doing it. If food is your thing, sitting in a room with people eating fish and chips; try not salivating and wanting to eat them, it's the same with alcohol and drugs (well not salivating, but you get my point).

Obviously this is easier for some things than others. Drugs can be slightly easier to avoid, because they are illegal they are not in your face most of the time, you just avoid the people you know that will be using the substance and the places where people might be using. This can be very successful in the early days. Because you are not seeing it, it's easier to stop. This can be hard though if you don't have any non-using friends. Then you really have to spend time building new social systems, work, training, volunteering, hobbies etc. where people will be, that are not drug users obviously.

Alcohol can be really tough for visual triggers. It's on the TV, films, adverts, in the supermarket, garage, it's pretty much everywhere.

I recently spent a few days in Spain and I swear to God, there was not a moment where I couldn't see a reference to alcohol, unless I was in my room. Adverts, cafes, bars, people drinking everywhere! So without really noticing you will see it, which may trigger a craving.

Although I didn't want to drink and had no intention to, I found myself for a moment thinking about it, seeing people sat in the bars drinking, I was like, oooh that looks nice, I could do that. Then I would shake it off. I thought it through. I don't drink very often anymore and as you know I did a long period with nothing and still do long periods with nothing. I didn't want to drink as my tolerance is so low now (which is good) that when I do have 1 drink, I know I have had a drink. I can really feel it and 1 is enough.

It's the same with food, junk food, sugar. Takeaways are everywhere, chocolate and sweets at the counter in the garage when you get petrol. Again, it's pretty impossible to avoid the visual trigger of junk and crappy foods. Unless you live in the middle of nowhere and only come into civilisation occasionally, then it's a lot easier.

I for one would love to see all advertising banned for anything that is bad for us.

No alcohol, takeaway, junk food, sugary food adverts anywhere, just imagine. I know some people will say well you just have to learn to moderate. Yes I agree we do need to do this. However many of us really struggle with this and obesity and alcohol are a massive drain on our health services. And really we don't need to advertise things that are bad for us. We don't see adverts for heroin or cocaine.

We know this has really worked with tobacco, no advertising, really clear about the health messages, so there are no inconsistent messages, confusing us. You can't see it very much at all. In fact it's only if you know a smoker or you smell someone walking down the road you come into contact with it anymore. Obviously putting the price up really helps to. Imagine a world where things that are good for you are advertised, lovely big bright visual images of fruit and veg.

This Too Shall Pass

We have established that cravings can happen for a multitude of reasons, there are many triggers internal and external. We can do something about the external triggers up to a point. Even then we won't eliminate them all. And remember that's normal, it's Ok, don't panic.

It's Ok.

The craving will pass. How long it takes will be dependent on the situation and why you are having the craving or, if there is a reason. Also how long you decide to stay in the craving will have an effect, yes some people just add to it and make it hard for themselves, latching onto it and really thinking about it. It could be seconds, minutes, but definitely no longer than 20 minutes, unless you are really good at staying in it.

So just wait and it will pass, ideally take you mind off it, then it will pass quicker.

Distraction, self-talk, talking it through with someone else or going through the consequences are good ways of dealing with a craving.

Say someone offers me a drink, a drug, a big sticky cake. If I stop, take a breath, and think it through, such as, if I have that drink will I stop at 1, probably not. Maybe I need to drive, do some work or I have to get up early in the morning. If I have more than 1, I will feel rough, do I want to feel rough or do I want to be on top of my game as I have a busy day tomorrow. I then start identifying with feeling good, that good feeling you have when you wake up and you haven't had a drink. Remember that feeling. Thinking through the consequences of your potential actions will really help manage the craving.

Having a goal can really help too, even if it's a small one. Knowing why you are doing this is really important. Daily motivation is a massive help, is your motivation about weight, how you feel, your work, parenting, money or your relationship?

Task: Take your mind of it.

You need to do something that changes how you feel.

Get a pen and paper and write down a list of things you can do. Examples include:

- Playing some music
- Playing with the children
- Cook
- Reading
- Have a bath
- Running
- Cycling
- Dance
- Walking the dog
- Cold shower

The list is endless, but it needs to be things that work for you personally. That interrupt how you feel.

Once you have your list keep it somewhere you can call upon whenever cravings strike. Your phone is a great place.

The trick is not acting on the craving, the same as the emotions we talked about earlier. Remember we said earlier, we experience a range of emotions throughout the day and we don't act on them all?

Some of the triggers may be some of the things we have talked about already in this book.

This could be a difficult job, relationships or life situations etc. You may already be working on these. So that will make it easier.

One of my triggers was my ex-husband and my youngest son's behaviour. After I had done the work on myself so that I didn't allow my ex-husband to get the better of me, that wasn't so much of a trigger anymore. Then after some time, with all the work we did, my youngest sons behaviour improved, so his behaviour is no longer a trigger either.

Tiredness and stress is a big trigger for a lot of people.

I really notice when I am tired and I have been tired for long periods that I have more cravings for junk food and for alcohol. So rather than reaching for the bottle I listen to myself and take some time out relaxing. This is much more beneficial.

I really notice this with a lot of the people I have worked with over the years. As we have said in the tiredness chapter, people underestimate the power of "just" being tired.

So make peace with cravings .

It's ok, we all have them.

You will may experience cravings for sometime and that's ok too.

It will get easier.

You will learn how to manage them better.

Understand your process, visual triggers, situations, people, events etc.

When you have one, it will pass – I guarantee it.

Sit with it.

Stop, breathe, and talk yourself through it. What will happen if you act on the craving? Consequences? How will you feel? What will happen next? How does that effect your day? Your tomorrow? Your current goal?

The one thing I can guarantee Is that everything will change.

If you are feeling bad, sit with it,
it wont kill you.
The feeling will pass.

20. Socialising without alcohol.

It can absolutely be done and I highly recommend it.

There are a few things to be aware of first.

If alcohol has been a serious issue for you, so serious health implications, serious Mental health issues, you have been physically addicted. Then wait until you feel ok to do this, make it easy on yourself. There are lots of ways to socialise where alcohol isn't the focus or readily available.

When I am talking about socialising I mean going out, being around people. There are so many ways you can do this. It doesn't have to mean, going to a bar, club, parties stuff like that.

The important things is that you still get out and about in someway. You need to interact with people, even if you are an introvert. Human connection is so important. Even if its just talking to dog walkers when you are out walking the dog. Or chatting to people at your yoga class. It doesn't have to be deep and meaningful, it can start small like this.

Practice interacting with people without alcohol.

And really, seriously most of you have been doing this anyway, at work probably. When you start a new job, lots of new people, most of you won't have had a drink. So there will be at least one scenario you can draw upon where you are mixing with people and not using alcohol.

Think about it differently.

Here are some tips on how to deal with social situations. Could be a family get together, or a work function. It doesn't have to be anything major. But it's going to happen.

- Choose your words wisely: Be armed with several different things you can say. It can be anything the important thing is you are comfortable with it. "I am on medication" is a good one, people don't argue with that. Be the driver, again no argument. "I am taking a break" (makes it sound temporary even if it's not). I want to lose some weight (again most people are supportive of this one). You are training for something (a particular exercise event like running etc.). These are a good few options. Make sure you have at least one you can use that you feel comfortable with. This will help you out in the first few weeks.

- Be honest: The other option if you are sure and you really want to put your money where your mouth is, is to say it outright: "I don't want to drink for a while." "It doesn't agree with me", "I don't like how I am when I drink", whatever the reason is for your change. This will stimulate some debate, so make sure you are ready for this.

- Be prepared. As we are a nation of drinkers, be ready for people not liking your choice. But you know what, here's the thing, it's your life, your choice. Personally, if someone really gives you a hard time about making a decision that's good for you that's really not very helpful or supportive. Surely if people care about you they are pleased that you are looking after yourself?

- Expect opposition: People prefer it if you all drink together, they are uncomfortable if someone chooses to be different, yet stay as part of the crowd. It's just different, everyone needs to get over it. In fact it's better to have someone sober around, if anything goes wrong there is someone there to help out that's capable.
- Be persistent: If you really want to do this, be prepared to persist and keep saying the same thing, having the same conversation. I think I did this for about the first year when I stopped drinking.
- Opt out of rounds, otherwise you have to deal with the question repeatedly.
- Drink soft drinks that could be anything. Sometimes no one will ask, as everyone assumes that everyone drinks.

If you notice you are staying at home a lot and not really getting out and about, well for many reasons. Maybe your social circle is all about alcohol so its easier to stay away for a while. You need to choose something you can do that means you will be around people. It can be anything, preferably something you enjoy. A hobby, an evening class, a sport, anything where there are people and the focus isn't booze.

When you go you may feel nervous, mostly people just feel different. You don't have to have had a problem with alcohol to find this challenging. Even people that think they don't have a problem, that take a break for a while, notice how different it is to socialise without alcohol.

Here is the thing, the feeling is different that's all. If you have always used alcohol when socialising this is a new experience. Feeling different wont kill you, alcohol will.

There are a few things you can do that will help.

- Pick an activity that doesn't revolve around alcohol.
- Whatever you do make sure its doing something, sitting and just talking can be tough for some people until they get used to it.
- Whatever you pick give it a chance, it takes time, to meet new people and bond when our favourite social lubricant isn't there to help.
- Try something for a couple of months, go every week, be consistent, smile at people, make small talk.
- Try different things until you find something you enjoy doing and you start to feel comfortable doing it without alcohol.
- Take the time to listen to people, when you focus on others it stops you thinking about you and how you are feeling.

If you read any of my blogs or participate in any of my on-line communities you will know that when I first stopped I went partner dancing. It worked really well for me. The focus isn't on alcohol, its fun, lots of people feel nervous because its dancing so you are not the only one. Because its dancing the focus isn't on conversation either, which is really helpful if you feel awkward. So I could go and dance, be with people, but not have to say a lot if I didn't want to. Somewhere to go, something to do that isn't about alcohol. Also it took time for me to make friends, I kept going, so it became familiar.

21. Just say "No" (sorry, couldn't resist that)

I am sure by now, you know what I am going to say here.

Just say No

It's cheesy but true.

No means No.

Just say it.

Seriously there are things you can do to help yourself and this is one of them.

Saying no when it is readily available. Means you will get well practiced at it. If you really can't avoid it or even restrict your availability.

The more you say no the easier it gets. It's like a muscle, the more you do squats the easier they are. After a while you actually get a boost from saying no. It feels good, check me out, refusing something that I don't want.

Recently I was with a friend of mine at a wedding, she is alcohol free and loving it. She has decided that alcohol adds nothing to her life at all and her intention is to remain alcohol free, she feels really good about it, her life has significantly improved. She is 100% clear why she isn't drinking and the benefits to her, so when she was offered a drink and she said, "no thanks, I don't drink" she said it with such conviction, such confidence, she looked really happy and pleased with her self too. The response was one of support because of the way she delivered the message.

There is something ingrained in us that we feel like we need to accept everything that is offered to us and we don't. Some cultures are set up so that you have to eat everything they give you, it's seen as being rude if you don't.

When I worked in India in my 20's I used to have dinner with the people I worked with and they would cook these amazing meals, that went on forever, and had things in it I had never seen or want to taste again.

It was a given that I would eat everything as it would be very rude if I didn't. I would be so ill for the next few days.

Telling friends, family, people who are in your life, what you are doing is a good idea. It puts it out there, you can see who will support you. You can actively ask people to support. E.g. If you have an event to go to, you can ask a good friend to come who will support you by not drinking.

If you tell people what you are doing and then ask for support, you naturally have to say no less. What you are looking for is people not even offering which makes life a lot easier.

If you struggle to say no, ask yourself why is that? Are you people pleasing? Are there people you struggle to say no to? Like your gran who has baked you a cake, that you don't want, but you can't say no, because she has spent time baking it and she hasn't seen you for ages, she would be offended if you didn't eat some.

The reality is there is always going to be 1 person you may have this problem with, can you avoid them early days? Sometimes I have taken the drink and then just not drunk it in these situations. They haven't even noticed. Just be careful with this one, because if its really important you stop drinking for physical health or mental health, life, reasons then you need to manage this one so it works for you. If its important you will need to speak to the person.

Avoidance

We really need to talk about this one. In the early days it may be easier to avoid certain situations until you feel ready. Yes you can say no but at the start it may be easier to avoid being asked at all. I see a lot of people challenging this. "You shouldn't avoid, you shouldn't have to change your life." I agree, sort of. But let's be real, the bottom line is it can be hard, if not almost impossible to not eat the sweets when you are living in the sweetie shop. So why would you do that to yourself?

It depends on the situation but try not to do this for too long.

If it's something that has been very serious for you, impact on your health, your relationship, finances, children, work. Then hell yes you need to stay away from anything that is going to be a problem.

One of my favourites used to be when someone makes changes to their drinking. They are doing well and are feeling so much better. Then they are talking about going back to work, or getting a part time job, in a bar. I mean really how long will you last not drinking? Who knows? But what you can be sure of is if you don't work in a bar you will have a better chance.

I am sure you get the point, sometimes we have to be real about these things.

The trick is to do something different so you don't feel like you are depriving yourself, avoiding, sacrifice, isolating, doing nothing. That's not the point of this, if you just stop drinking even if its for a month and change nothing, you wont really feel the benefits.

22. Extra bits

Sticking to it.

Some people find it easy to start, but then after a few days the motivation momentum has gone.

Things won't change unless you stick at it, keep going, and persist.

People do well at things: work, careers, training, sport, parenting, any area of life that you can think of. They do well because they focus on it. They listen and they learn from people who have been successful in the chosen area.

So, if you want this to work, you have to put the work in. When you want a new job you spend time researching, writing, editing your C.V., meeting people, it takes time, but you keep going, because that's what you want, it's your focus.

If you want to pass an exam, you revise, you read and focus.

If you are training for an event, such as a 5k. You run regularly, you build up your strength and you think about what you are eating etc.

My point is if you want something you have to put the effort in. Now it's not a huge amount of effort and time. And the reason why I have written this book and developed different programmes is because I want you to have access to lots of different tips and techniques that will help you along the way. Things you can integrate into your everyday life.

Make yourself do something towards it every day. Even if it's something little, the more you do it the easier it will become. Make it a priority, prioritize you.

When people get out of the habit of exercise and they are not doing anything, a good trainer worth their salt, will encourage you to do just 10mins of exercise every other day. Just to get you started, to get the muscles going, to start the habit, before long you will be doing 30 mins and so on.

Persist, keep going.

I regularly hear people want quick results when it comes to this particular issue: drugs, drink, food etc. It can be quick if you put the time and effort in, but it's not going to happen overnight.

I commonly hear from people that are maybe 2 weeks in, things are going well. They have made some changes. Maybe even stopped what was causing them a problem and just had a couple of blips. Anyway it's all good and they are moving in the right direction. They are struggling emotionally – this can be normal. They are making changes, focusing on things they might have been masking or running from. They can be giving themselves a hard time, wanting to be fixed now. We don't expect this in any other are of your lives, so why do we do it here?

This is most common and obvious when there has been a serious issue around addiction. When someone is a heavy drinker or drug user. They have stopped its early days and its tough. They are learning new things and life is changing rapidly, the comfortable slipper is gone, and everything feels new and awkward. I encourage people to think of it the same as if you have been ill. If you go to hospital and have an operation, or you have had a virus and been ill, you give yourself time to recover. You may not want to take 6 weeks off or however long the doctor has said you need to take but you do your best to take it easy relax. You cut yourself some slack, maybe for even longer.

So this is the same, particularly if you have been a heavy or regular user. In the early days be nice to yourself. Sleep, eat healthy, do nice things, stop giving yourself a hard time. You are on the right track.

Anything that you have taken excessively that is bad for you, your body and brain will need time to recover from. Cocaine is particularly difficult in the early days maybe even 3 months.

The way cocaine works in the brain with your dopamine receptors means that when you stop, everything can feel numb for some time. While your brain re-adjusts to normal life and activities. Cocaine makes things feel good, temporarily. So when you stop everything can feel mundane, empty and robot like.

I call this the robot phase, it happens after quite a few different substances. You take the thing away that you have been using that gives you pleasure, particularly the ones that give you the dopamine, serotonin buzz. Then it can feel empty for some time.

Depending on how and why you drink alcohol. Alcohol can do this as well. When you first stop, you miss the pleasure buzz, "what's the point?" you think. **It won't last, ride it out, I promise it will be worth it.**

Food does this as well, if you are an eater that eats the junk, rubbishy, sugary food. When you eat it you get a serotonin buzz. You eat the cake, you feel nice for a minute, and then you want to repeat the feeling. When you consciously take a break or stop eating the rubbishy things that have no nutritional value, you need to get your serotonin buzz from elsewhere.

Normal activities that would normally give pleasure don't for you. The only thing to do here is to ride it out. Your brain will reset itself. Using again to get the pleasure is only going to prolong the inevitable. And you do want your life to be different right? So you just have to go through that phase.

Remember you have been using the quick fix, the not-so-magic button. I want to feel a certain way therefore if I use this, drink, drug, food, it will change how I feel quickly. And it does, it's that instant reward, instant gratification. Be aware of this, just accept that for a while (probably only a short time, months at the most) that you are learning to find other ways to get your feels and it won't happen overnight. So put the instant gratification to bed while you are learning this. It's OK, it won't kill you not to have the instant gratification.

What's really great is that when it does come back and it will. You find yourself gaining pleasure from the simplest of things. The natural high that people talk about is there and it is amazing.

Have a listen to my podcast extra ordinary people no 1. Vicky talks about that, how she feels euphoria nothing like she has ever experienced without the aid of any substances.

https://www.ichange21.com/blog/extra-ordinary-people-podcast-1

Having a bad day or a bad week.

Ok, here's the thing, we have talked a lot about stress and things going wrong or not working in our life. When you stop, take a break, give up, and reduce, whatever you decide to do. I can guarantee you that something is going to happen that will piss you off, little or big. It will. It could be work, stress, family, friends etc and all the other things we have talked about. This is part of life and learning to deal with these things without reaching for your preferred drug is important. Accepting that you are human is important and you are going to have bad days/weeks. Its ok, life happens, it's not perfect.

I quite often get people coming to me with problems and asking for help saying they feel terrible and want to feel better, when they tell me what the problem is its normal for them to feel bad.

I think we are tough on ourselves. It's ok to have a bad day and feel rubbish. It's then what you do with it that matters, avoid going back to the instant gratification. Learning new habits to help you in these moments is essential. That's why I bang on about sport, hobbies etc.

And you may say god I am not sporty at all, that's ok, you will have something you can do. You may have just forgotten: reading, walking, being in nature, yoga, there are lots of things you can do. But sometimes you have to force yourself.

Realising you Have One

If you have got this far in the book, you will know by now if it's a problem for you or not.

Be clear what the problem is. Why is it a problem for you? This will help you stay on track.

I met a lovely woman the other day. And as usually happens, when we get on the subject of what I do for work, she started telling me her story. She told me about her drinking and how much she enjoyed it. She was honest in saying that sometimes she drank regularly and sometimes she binged and yes sometimes she danced on the tables (which incidentally I don't think is a bad thing, the dancing on tables that is). However, she was very clear in that it wasn't a problem for her. She knew it was a phase and at some point she would grow out of it.

And she did. Drink was no longer part of her life for no reason other than it held no interest for her anymore. She had this theory that people would eventually just grow out of it.

I explained to her that people come to me because there is a problem, they might not know what it is, but it's causing them a problem. Whether it's their health, emotions, relationships, money, work, children etc. Something isn't working and they want to change it. This almost always involved reducing, gaining control or stopping whatever the bad habit is.

For her as she said it just wasn't a problem.

If there is a problem, be honest with yourself.

The moment I realised, was when I was in custody and it was my fault. Before that I wasn't really paying attention at all. I sort of knew I could be out of control. Emotionally, for myself and for others and that wasn't ok. But I wasn't really thinking it through, otherwise I wouldn't have done some of the things I did and taken the risks I had.

So, I was honest. The only person that was responsible for me being arrested was me. No one else. It wasn't the police's fault for picking on me, I had committed a crime. They were doing their job. It wasn't my ex-husbands fault either. It was mine, I was drinking too much as well as other things and taking risks and I had been caught. Then I had to ask myself how I had got there. How had I allowed things to get so out of control and not notice?

I played my life in my head and saw the roller coaster, up and down, in and out, hanging on, doing well, and pretending. It was just a matter of time and could have happened anytime from 18 onwards.

Lillie says, in her podcast. The start for her, was being honest with herself and then asking for help. Being honest that things had got out of control.

https://www.ichange21.com/blog/extra-ordinary-people-podcast-2

Sometimes I start working with people and they start off by not being that honest about their behaviour or how much they are drinking etc. After a couple of weeks, they feel able to say it as it is. It feels horrible sometimes I know, to own it, say it out loud it can be embarrassing. It can also feel liberating to just say it.

If it feels horrible and makes you squirmy, you don't have to keep saying it and reliving the horrible feeling. Just admit to yourself there is a problem, what it is and then start to address it.

Emotional and Physical Well-being

I cannot stress to you how important this is, I think I make that absolutely clear throughout the whole book. This is your life, your brain and your body. Look after it. It will work better, be more useful to you and life will be more enjoyable. The more you look after it the more you can do. Back to the car analogy. You keep it clean, you service it, and you change the oil, keep it topped up with water, and if things break you repair them. If you don't it just doesn't work as well or not at all.

One of the days learning in the Stop Drinking and Start Living online coaching programme, talks about the importance of looking after yourself: sleep, water, regular healthy food, exercise etc. They are the basics, the ground work, the fundamentals of life, the building blocks. You don't have to do it all the time, but a good 90% will really reap the rewards.

Laying the Groundwork.

I worked with Sarah and she was quite depressed. He wasn't really sure what was happening. She was really struggling with her emotions and this was a new thing for her. Normally she was quite resilient and positive, coping with life well.

All of a sudden she was struggling to sleep, crying, feeling very low, hopeless, anxious, paranoid, a whole range of feelings. She was depressed.

We unpicked what was happening. I asked her those key questions. Alcohol ? drugs? Life? She confessed to pretty much always drinking. She had been drinking regularly for the last 20 years at least and always had the odd binge. Sometimes she would drink everyday for long periods of time. As we all know alcohol is a depressant and the side-effects are disrupted sleep, anxiety and paranoia. So this level of alcohol use is going to have a repercussion at some point, physically or emotionally. Then she told me that she had been taking party drugs since a teenager. Having fun, party's festivals, pretty much all her adult life.

As I have said previously when taking different substances, the brains reaction to big increases in dopamine is often to reduce the number of functioning dopamine receptors leading to a reduced sense of reward from other activities and greater dependence on the drug. Hence it goes around and around.

It's quite normal for people to feel depressed after using party drugs and if you are a regular user then there will definitely be a repercussion at some point, physical or emotional. Depending on how resilient you are in each area.

Before we even started on what was happening in her life, a recent family bereavement, trouble with a family member, lots of changes at home and her partner having problems. I was not surprised that she was depressed.

However, working with her, for her to be realistic about what had caused it was very interesting. She didn't want to acknowledge that her using had contributed to how she was feeling. I put it to her that she might have struggled anyway with all these life events, however with her past and current using, that would exacerbate her emotional health for sure.

For her to feel better she would need to cut out all the drinking and partying for 3 months (at least). Maybe even have some anti-depressants and then get some support.

So, if you are drinking, using drugs and struggling emotionally and physically. I can't stress to you how important it is to cut the drink and drugs. Get some support with that, look after yourself and then see how you feel.

Fear and Procrastination

Mostly when people get to me they are ready, they have thought about their life being different, they want to change, they may not know how or why. However, some people want their lives to be different but they are scared, petrified even. They are unsure of what the future holds and what will happen without their crutches.

I am a big fan of feel the fear and do it anyway. Fear is just a feeling although a powerful one, but it won't kill you. And actually, the more you do something the less fear you feel.

Speaking in public, even in small groups, even just speaking up, most people find mortifying. However, the more you do it the easier it gets. Unless you are very anxious and sometimes it gets worse, then you really need some coaching to stop this, if you need to speak up that is.

Sometimes we are just scared of the unknown. Here's the thing, you don't know what is going to happen anyway. Really you don't.

If you are scared of feeling different – yes you will feel different. Again it's a feeling it won't kill you, sit with it, you won't feel like that forever. The one thing I can guarantee is that everything will change.

Another way of looking at this is, what will happen if you don't change?

Saying to Yourself It is Forever

This is a big one and we have talked about language. You might need to say its forever, that might work for you. However, saying its forever might make it harder for you to make changes. It's your language, it makes sense to you, don't worry if others don't get it, it's your journey not theirs.

I see a lot of things written, you must abstain, you can't moderate etc. etc. you know how it goes. Mostly people are writing about what has worked for them. Which is great, it's great to share when something has worked for you. Please remember though that everyone is different, which is one of the many reasons why I have written this book.

It's based on working with 1000's of people. It maybe that I can teach you 20 different ways, techniques, methodologies, within that there will be something, a couple of things that really resonate and work for you.

This is the same when we talk about whether you are giving up, taking a break, needing to be abstinent, reducing, moderating, controlling. These words mean different things to different people.

People who have had a serious problem, it's been life threatening, they have lost a lot, at risk of losing things important to them, used excessively. These people probably need to say, I need to be abstinent.

Otherwise use words that work for you.

Find other ways of feeling happy

So important and sometimes this one takes time. Be patient.

If it happens quickly and you find other things that make you feel happy, great. Do them regularly and keep doing them, use them as your thing, your happy place.

You have an argument or an altercation with someone. You feel hurt upset, you want to change the feeling, you don't want to feel like that, the feeling is hanging around you, you can't shake it off. You want to drink, take something, eat something as that will change how you feel and make you feel better (in the short term) different. Quick fix, bad habit.

Back to the magic button.

You can find other magic buttons, healthy ones, and ones that are good for you. They may require a lot more effort initially, but they are worth it.

Sometimes it takes time, to find something and you can feel cold, robot like, as if there is no joy in your life, what's the point. I can remember someone telling me that they didn't want to give up smoking as it was the only thing that gave them pleasure in their life.

Be patient. It will happen, you will find something that makes you happy.

Happy people live quite simple lives, they sleep well, eat healthy, they don't sweat the small stuff.

They don't take things personally, they have things in perspective. It doesn't mean they are perfect, they are more able to let things go.

"There are over 7 billion people on earth and you are going to let 1 person ruin your day?"

It's not rocket science, it really isn't. Keep it simple, don't overcomplicate things its isn't necessary.

- Keep it simple, this is so important.
- The happiest people in the world keep it simple and have simple lives.
- Nothing needs to be complicated, don't over complicate things, there is always an easier way.
- When things get tough, strip it back, keep it simple.
- "When you are overwhelmed, tired or stressed the solution is almost always less. Get rid of something, lots of somethings."
- Sleep, eat healthy, exercise, be with people who love you, relax.

Do Something

you love.

I don't know anyone that has made changes to their bad habits whatever they are and have come back to see me and told me their life is terrible or far worse that it was when they were, drinking, taking drugs, eating too much.

No one. Not even when I worked in a drug and alcohol treatment service. People might have struggled in the first few months but if they followed all the advice, which would help them and learnt new habits, then they felt better.

Even if people don't keep in contact with me regularly, I get random messages, 1 year 2 years later telling me how much better their lives are, how they feel more in control and feel happier.

I see people regularly in the street my teams worked with years ago and they love to stop and tell me how much better their life is.

Nobody has ever stopped me to tell me their life is worse since giving up.

Letting go

I think it's clear throughout the book, staying in the past isn't going to help you. You can't change the past, I have said it a lot and I will keep saying it. People stay in the negative emotion of events that have happened, whether it's is something they have caused or something that just happened because of others.

We have talked about right and wrong, its mostly irrelevant. Obviously there are situations, where things have gone wrong and it needs to be dealt with and this can take time. Court cases etc. If this is the case it's hard not to revisit what has happened. Look after yourself.

Let go of the negative emotion.

This quote explains it well and simply.

"Holding on to anger is like grasping a hot coal with the intent of throwing it at someone else, you are the one that gets burned".

It can be any negative emotion.

If you need to talk about it, to let it go and to process it that's fine. Go and see a counsellor. Counselling will allow you to just sit and talk. Again, though if you keep talking about it why? What are you hoping to gain from repeating the experience, because that's what you do? When you think about it and talk about it, you experience it on some level revisiting the negative emotion.

Are you punishing yourself?

If you keep experiencing the negative emotion and you are unable to let it go and you want to. Please go and see a good coach. They will be able to work with you, so you can move on.

I have worked with many people who are punishing themselves, not consciously of course.

But when we really look at what is happening, that's what it comes down to. And it's generally for something that happened way in the past that quite often other people have forgotten about, or maybe it wasn't so important to them.

A divorce from years ago, that split a family up, upset the children and hurt the other partner.

Using substances, drinking, or spending money, that effects the family.

Decisions we make that affect others.

Not being there when someone really needed us.

The list is endless.

So many reasons to stay in the past, beat ourselves up, replay events over and over. Or even just feeling vindicated because you were right and they were wrong.

YOU CAN'T CHANGE IT.

Isn't it better to learn from it, let it go and move on?

"Acceptance and forgiveness is linked to motivation"

Accept it, if you can't change it.

If you can't accept it, you need to ask yourself why and again do the work with a coach.

Then if you can, forgive yourself and others if necessary.

Sometimes its useful to accept that people are doing the best they can with what they have. I really believe this. We are all different. Don't expect others to live and understand the way you live and abide by your code and values etc.

Sometimes it can be hard to forgive others, particularly if it has caused a very serious event.

I worked with a woman who had been in an abusive marriage and it had taken her a long time to get out of it. Then the abuse just continued. It went on for years and years in many different forms. The effect on herself and her children was very difficult. She had to work hard to keep it all together. After time, she was able to see that he wasn't going to change. He couldn't, that was just the way he was, he would probably be like that forever. It wasn't personal she just got caught in the crossfire, he is like that with all women. Once she accepted his behaviour, it allowed her to let go of a lot of things. It no longer had a grip on her in the way he wanted. It made things a lot easier to manage and she was able to move on with her live. It freed her up from being in that negative space.

I know this may sound like a stretch. But I really need you to understand this. If she carried on the way she was, scared, anxious, dealing with it every day. The only person that lost was her and her children. She would get ill, probably use alcohol, drugs, shorten her life significantly and also it is a miserable way to live. By letting it all go, accepting he wasn't going to change and learning how to live so it didn't affect her was liberating.

Let it go.

What are you hanging on to?

That if you let go, now, today, would free you up to be able to live your life?

What's stopping you, from letting it go?

3 solutions to every problem

"Accept it, change it, or leave it. If you can't accept it, change it, if you can't change it leave it."

ACCEPTANCE

&

FORGIVENESS

is linked to motivation.

Dalai Lama

Guilt and Shame.

A little word about Guilt and Shame.

We have spoken already about negative emotions, negative self talk. This is part of that.

Some people experience terrible guilt and shame and this feels awful. Now there are a few tricky bits here that go with this.

What can happen is there is an event or events that people feel bad about, feel guilty and shameful. You can't change the past, you can't go back and do it differently. Trust me I wish you could. So then why are you giving yourself a hard time about something in your past you can't change?

I want you to answer that question, its important.

Usually people are punishing themselves, they feel unable to move on in their life because they feel they don't deserve to because of what they have done in their past.

There are a number of ways of tackling this. You can talk it out until you feel better, usually this may involve speaking to the people involved.

There are a few things to remember here. How you remember things is your reality. We create our own realities. So how the event or events are to you, will be different to the other people. That's the first point to consider, sometimes you will talk to someone and they have a completely different take on it. The other things is the person may not want to discuss it, or hear what you have to say, for many reasons. None of which may be about you.

Also it may be more painful for the other person, if this is possible please consider this very carefully. Remember this is your guilt and shame and yes great you want to do something about it, but not at the expense of others.

So many things to consider here, however don't let that put you off, just make sure you are making a considered decision. It can and does go well for a lot of people.

Personally, myself when I have done this, apologised for my behaviour, I have chosen my time, picked my opportunity and gauged whether it's an ok thing for each party. It hasn't always gone well either and I have had to accept that some of the things in my past have been quite difficult for other people in my life.

You can go and see a counsellor and talk through your feelings about past events, which can be useful as you get an objective point of view. Sometimes people feel bad about things that on the grand scale of things aren't that much of an issue, they are just giving themselves a hard time, back to the punishing.

You can see a good coach or therapist and really work through letting it go.

The key bit here is its in the past, you can't change it, you can change your today, your behaviour, your choices. You can be a different person. Showing people you are different is as powerful if not more so than our words.

23. Why am I making such a big deal about alcohol

Alcohol is our most commonly used substance. Not only that it is one of our most harmful. When we talk about harm, it's the physical harm to the individual, emotional harm and social harms.

For instance, heroin causes problems to the community in terms of the repetitive low level crime that a heavy heroin user may commit to fund their habit. As well as the wider issues of drug trafficking and the huge amount of crime associated with this. If the user injects the heroin this also has massive physical harms for the individual, risk of overdose, health, injecting any drug is very high risk for an individual's health. If a person becomes addicted to heroin it can have serious long term impact on all areas of their life. It's clear that heroin (and cocaine) are one of our most harmful substances and I don't think that anyone would disagree with this.

The thing is we all know that, we know the risks. Very few people will even try heroin. Our using heroin population is decreasing, in fact we have an ageing population of heroin users in the UK.

When it comes to alcohol the information hasn't been so clear and we can all be forgiven if we are a little confused, so much mis information out there.

Alcohol is harmful to the individual physically and emotionally. If you are a regular user of alcohol the physical effects are huge and effect every part of your body. As well as emotional effects, depression, paranoia, anxiety and so on. Alcohol also effects our community. Not in the same ways as heroin and cocaine, purely because alcohol is legal. However anyone can see any Friday and Saturday night in any British town or city the cost, to the individual and community. The cost of policing drunk people, sometimes violence. How it effects relationships, parenting, career, business, I could go on.

This is why I go on about alcohol. I want you to be aware, educated, I want you to be able to make an informed choice. Like you do about heroin. I bet most of you, if you were at a party and was offered some heroin you would say no.

Alcohol is socially acceptable and I don't think that is going to change anytime soon. It is getting better, there are more coffee bars, alcohol free drinks etc. There is a movement of lots of different people, business's like myself, encouraging and promoting good information.

Alcohol is the one I want you to know about, be aware of.

All the information and tasks in this book can easily apply to any other substance or problem. Such as tobacco, gambling, cocaine.

Important note if you are a regular user of, or experiencing problems with opiate based pain killers and/or benzodiazepines, please go and see your doctor.

These substances are physically and psychologically addictive and you will need support from your doctor to reduce slowly. Benzodiazepines carry significant risks in terms of withdrawal.

Cannabis, acid, ecstasy, ketamine, mushrooms, these substances are a lot less harmful. It doesn't mean that people don't have issues with them. But it's usually a lot less of an issue. For instance, it's unlikely you are going to become addicted to acid or mushrooms, in all my years I don't think I have ever met in my personal or professional life someone with a dependency problem with hallucinogens. The problems that can happen with these substances are more likely in that they don't agree with the person, or they experience bad trips. If you take something and you don't like it, I would expect that you don't take it again. It's fairly simple.

Sometimes people try it a few times, but if it's not working for them they usually stop.

If you are taking something that you don't have a good experience with, or doesn't agree with you and you continue doing this, you need to ask yourself some serious questions and I highly recommend you get some support from a good coach with a lot of addiction experience.

24. Top tips from others

In this book is a lot of information to help you make changes. I hope that something resonates with you. All it takes is one thing to get you started, then use the other bits to keep going.

People make changes everyday. I meet people all the time that are working to live the life they want. All sorts of people from all walks of life. I have seen people make amazing transformations and go onto do amazing things. Anything is possible ☺

If one person can do it, you can.

Here are some top tips from people who have made big changes and are still living happy healthy lives.

"Distance yourself from the environments in which you would be around any bad temptations. "

"Anything in recovery is better than nothing...you are still closer to achieving your goal than you were before...do not let one slip up break all your hard work, you are doing so well just put it behind you and keep going. (Depending on circumstance... I got told when I had a setback to use it as a good thing- as it showed me how bad it used to make me feel, and the behaviour that I used to do... and it reminded me that I didn't want to slip back into that pattern again. This was then a good anchor to avoid repeating the behaviour to avoid the unwanted feelings/ outcome. (Hope this makes sense) ".

"Reach out to others with your struggles, you will see you are not alone ".

"Keeping a journal or an accountability partner ".

"See it as a complete lifestyle change. Buy into it fully. Feel the success and visualise it."

"Keep telling yourself that it's easy, you can do this. The basic things in life that you need to survive are food and water. Don't let that little monster inside you try and convince you otherwise. Be strong and believe in yourself- your loved ones do! "

"You have to want to do it, I don't think it works when imposed. "

"Keep trying and don't give up ".

"See yourself as someone who doesn't do what it is you are trying to change. i.e. - Why would I smoke, I'm a non-smoker. Make every step a step towards your goal as often as you can."

"Things do get better, sometimes you just have to hang in there and wait ".

"Change a little tiny bit at a time so as not to get overwhelmed."

"Trust that time will reveal a favourable outcome in your life. Just take that first step on the journey of change".

"Take one day at a time ".

"Never, ever touch one bite, one drink or one puff ever again ".

"When you feel the need to do whatever it is, give yourself 10 minutes to consider the pros and cons. If that is hard to do on your own, arrange for a friend to talk to on the phone ".

"Think about what you get out of the thing you want to stop doing and meet that need another way ".

"It's in the mind. Be strong and be patient ".

"Change your way of thinking. You need a new set of eyes, ears and thought processes. It is largely learnt behaviour and therefore can be unlearnt ".

"Meditate ".

"Find the root cause of what troubles you and thus pushes you to addiction".

"Take it slowly. One win at a time ".

"That a craving is evidence of the habit you are trying to break - and that therefore what you are doing is necessary and worthwhile - a craving is evidence of you beating it- it is evidence of the habit trying to maintain itself and losing.... "

"Just do it. Take action and then keep going, and learn what works for you. Build a life you love "

"I just found this poem I wrote a few years ago, when my life was pretty shit.... I kinda felt like there wasn't a way out of that, as many times can feel when you are down and it feels like this is just how life is and will be... however, it did change...diamonds can be fixed, healed and re-polished... if life is shit, and it feels like there is no way out. Really just remember, this will pass. YOU can do anything - if you put your mind to it. it requires some strength, determination and support (thank you, you know who you are) but from the bottom of my heart and truthfully ..... it will be ok xx"

The Invisible Diamond...

The Invisible Diamond is in the rough,
her light has dimmed, she ain't so tough.
In all her glory she once shined
now, not even one facet, you can find.
Her points that once were sharp as wit,
now blunt as night and dimly lit.

The invisible diamond has lost her way,
and dreams of sparkling like before that day.
In all her glory she once shined,
now people look through her like they were blind.
Her facets that once were sharp and new,
are cracked and torn and damaged through.
Nobody wants this flawed gem,
to look at her saddens them.
They can see who she once was,
and they know what she has lost.

The invisible diamond, what can she do?
she's just not fixable with needle nor glue.

No one is coming
to Save you.
This life is 100%
Your responsibility

About the Author

Stephanie Chivers is an expert in addictions and behaviour change. She is the curator, coach of the amazing Women Who Don't Drink group on Facebook. She has created affordable on-line coaching programmes that teach people how to stop drinking and change their life. She also provides 1-1 coaching, support for business's, training and speaking to promote health and educate about addiction and habit.

Stephanie is a master practitioner of NLP and coaching, she has worked within housing, mental health and drug and alcohol treatment services. She has worked as a support worker, practitioner, group worker, family worker, trainer, team leader and manager. She has a vast range of experience of working within the supporting people field. Supporting people to fulfil their potential as well as effecting change within other senior managers to improve service delivery for the people that need it.

References and Resources

What is NLP – "NLP is the study of excellence and how to reproduce it".
John Grinder, co-founder NLP.

In a world of change, more and more people are realising that their success, satisfaction and fulfilment in life, personally and professionally, can be influenced by themselves- and that the skills to achieve this can be learned.

When it comes to the field of personal and interpersonal skills development, NLP is at the cutting edge. NLP offers powerful yet simple and practical step-by-step methods for developing your skills in communication, self-awareness and personal development. NLP can be used for achieving positive results in almost any area of human experience.

The name NLP describes the interconnectedness of our neurological processes (Neuro) to language (Linguistic) and that these processes have a particular organization (Programming) that affects our behaviour.

"The most powerful tools, that I know of, for defining human needs and being able to fill those needs quickly and elegantly come from the technology known as NLP."
Anthony Robbins

What is coaching

There is no agreed definition of Life Coaching. However, it is often comprised of the following:

A professional relationship – a practice that helps people identify personal and professional goals.

Motivational interviewing.
A solution focused approach.
Support that focuses on achieving positive results.
Techniques and strategies to help you move forward in your life.
A holistic approach.

Information about alcohol

https://www.drinkaware.co.uk/

Is probably my favourite go to website for alcohol education and information. It's well presented and it's easy to navigate and find what you want. If you want to learn more about how it effects people, this is a good place to start.

https://www.alcoholconcern.org.uk/

Is the best place to go for the latest research if you are interested.

Information about drugs

I tend to find a lot of drug information sites tend to come from the perspective that all drugs are bad. Rather than factual based. Effects, potential harms etc. Some are better than others. As I have said before anything by Professor David Nutt is great factual information.

I also use a website called Erowid. https://www.erowid.org/ As well as Drugwise. http://www.drugwise.org.uk/drugsearch-encyclopedia/

Support

There are a few Facebook groups out there now. Check out:

Women Who Don't Drink.

Club Soda.

There are 12 step groups everywhere all around the world. They are free. There is a 12-step group for every type of addiction you can think off. The model is religious, spiritual and focussed around abstinence. The approach isn't for everyone. However, if you have a serious problem, it's worth a look. I personally like the steps, however the ethos isn't for me. I have seen it work for some people. Each group is different so it's worth trying a few before you make your mind up.

Search 12 step on line, or any Alcoholics anonymous, narcotics anonymous groups and go from there.

Smart recovery is pretty new for the UK. Depending on where you live will depend on whether there are any meetings. They may not be that regular. You can find them on line. They are solution focussed peer led groups and should be free as well. It's an alternative to a 12-step group, if you like attending groups with others with similar issues. There is also a Smart recovery in USA and Australia.

Relationship counselling. Try Relate in your area. Again, this all depends on the counsellor. It's about finding the right one for you. Don't be scared of asking for a different one until you find someone you can work with. If you want to go down the private route have a look on line. Any good coach, counsellor worth their salt will offer a free consultation before you pay for anything. This is so they can see if they can help as well as you seeing if you like them.

Other references in the book.

http://www.nhs.uk/Livewell/weight-loss-guide/Pages/calorie-counting.aspx
information about healthy eating and weight, with links.

Watch Cocaine unwrapped it tells you everything you need to know about the cocaine trade and may help motivate you to stop.
https://www.amazon.co.uk/dp/B01BUS00R8/ref=cm_sw_r_fa_dp_HztAyb47V7C07

Read, Drugs without the hot air by Professor David Nutt.

Read, Bronnie Wares blog about the 5 regrets of the dying
http://www.huffingtonpost.com/bronnie-ware/top-5-regrets-of-the-dyin_b_1220965.html
I can't publish it in the book due to copyright restrictions.

This book is for you if you want to change your relationship with alcohol, if you want your life to be different, to be better, feel healthier, happier, have better relationships, and fulfil your potential. If you believe in life and people, believe in our own abilities to change, the strength of the human spirit and a little bit of magic.

Printed in Great Britain
by Amazon

48137073R00155